AGE OF Innocence

Early Life and Times of Robin Blessed - Part One

ROBIN P. BLESSED

PARTRIDGE
A Penguin Random House Company

ISBN:	Hardcover	978-1-4828-9429-5
	Softcover	978-1-4828-9428-8
	Ebook	978-1-4828-9202-4

To order additional copies of this book, contact
Toll Free 800 101 2657 (Singapore)
Toll Free 1 800 81 7340 (Malaysia)
orders.singapore@partridgepublishing.com

www.partridgepublishing.com/singapore

Dedicated to all readers . . .

CONTENTS

INTRODUCTION

T o live without contemplating the events and experiences we passed through, is like the *walking dead*, merely—of flesh, of breath, and of the soul. Life is just skin-deep and material. Failure to consider and contemplate on events and experiences, their consequences, effects, influences, their lessons, their offered insights, leads to a superficial appreciation of who we are in the bigger plan of things: the *natural and humanly possible* in contrast to the *supernatural and humanly impossible*. We become strangely ignorant of our own heart, our own being. We live, we exist, we move, but know not who we are, what we truly perceive and think in those events of our lives. They are not merely about our self, but about us, and our space—our relationships to those about us—in our generation, in the next and beyond. Meditation and contemplation are like windows of light that flood the depths of our conscious mind as blood flushes red our pallid flesh, beholding the Truth lying inert as in comatose, and in a moment awaken our sensibility to it. Reflection is like a helicopter, when on the ground sees the immediately visible trees and objects; as it rises it sees more such as monkeys in the trees, a track leading out of the woods, no longer just the trees perceived earlier. The higher it rises it sees the overall *geography* of water and physical terrain, the trees that had become a forest and now patches of green, the '*communication*' of tracks and roads, a concept of the *social* and possibly *economic* milieu in the structure and density of dwellings. Events work with time and space to allow life to speak to us, in and through the issues, of the outlook. Contemplation puts that collaboration to work. Someone once said that '*life is not a little bundle of big things; it is a big bundle of little things*'.

This book is one about 'little things', of events rather than a continuous story, threaded together contiguously with the aid of chronology. Time is beautiful and yet not fully understood, a 'sticky' *intelligent* device of sorts, a fixed rigid scale—in what we can perceive and move in—on which man marks what enters upon his life against the time unit. Events come and go. Time faithfully and relentlessly marches on. As soon as a child is born, someone dies. Time . . . is life. *As thy days, so thy strength* . . . Time sets *history* in order, and gives it meaning. Time is certainty of the past. Yet history does not make the man, it is man who makes history. This book attempts to cast chronological events as a means to moderate a halting sense of my early life and times.

This is a book about my *growing up years* from more or less age 3: the earliest I can remember of an *event*, up until age 12, the logical transition to another phase in my life. My early years were symbolic of movement, of change. One thing after another seemed to come on incessantly and life was always full of the present: embracing its offerings, hopeful . . . every day I woke up to brand new frontiers of unexplored happenings, new vistas of enticing challenges, new hopes for the picking. They, like beautiful gifts from afar, must be unwrapped immediately and inspected with great expectancy. *Something* endlessly kept the spirits up, always up, always testing despite the physical and age limitations, amidst mostly brief experiences of anxiety, awe, humiliation, embarrassment, and trepidation. Unhappiness I knew not, as I did not understand happiness. I understood what was the present, the here, the now . . . today. There was not time for tomorrow until tomorrow comes along. All was just an experience, a passing one, much like an "aha" and then I am off to seek more. The agenda was a simple one: living the moment. That moment is not merely of an activity though seeming like passive idle 'watching', yet with lively observation, and active mental and emotional engagement.

Long before the idea of this book, I sought to understand how the *diverse* events in the *universe* of my life served a *purpose* if ever there was one. We do not exist for the sake of existing. Endowed with a complete range of our senses we experience all that we have been through and will go through in life, not merely for an existential motive that repulses any logic of meaning and purpose. Today I know assuredly that life did not just happen. For me, time brings a convergence of all events that dovetail or integrate into the ultimate web of life—a blueprint of purpose and destiny—that I now see of their coherence.

This book is not a product of creative writing. Each chapter carries a narrative report of an *event* from the eyes of a child. Children do not carry in their heads a continuous capture of life happenings like a running movie. Instead, they have a rich supply of short clips about events in their lives that may or may not be highly organised. Neither was the *additional information* presented, of the imagination, nor the outcomes, of invention.

I have frequently played back these events, turned them over often enough in my consciousness to understand them, very unlike analysis. *Reflection* and meditative contemplation better describes my intent.

I have often wondered how events *silently* and *unobserved* etched themselves into my personality and character. We have all been as clay in the invisible Potter's hands and the Potter's care and skill brings the clay to life, shaping every line and curve—all purposeful—to define us individually unique. Clay left to itself is just clay. In the events, I cannot claim to have any hand but I can be pliable for the Potter's use.

Reflection causes *outward* wonder—the awe of the Designer in His boundless space, one we are still seeking to reverently comprehend—therefore is pure and simple; analysis, on the other hand, imposes our limited experiences, confined prior knowledge with unexplained preferences, learnt prejudices, bred predispositions, and ungrounded opinions that intermeddle with an underlying *inward* self-centredness. Reflection had taught me to be grateful for all that came upon me—my birth into a great family of relationships, and the events that they enriched. They were all means for no personal selfish end in mind, no private agenda. Simply, they were valuable gifts to strengthen the heart to meet life in all its dimness, harshness, and seeming disparities, to render the heart tender where true relationships and feelings mattered over things and the pursuit of them.

Reflection is like to *commune with your own heart upon your bed, and be still* for in your bed, when all is quiet, you are alone free from activities that distract . . . you can talk only to yourself, to your own heart, truthfully. As looking in a mirror, you know what you see; as in your beating heart, what you hear; as in your resonating mind, what you think; and in contemplating, what you perceive and feel. No one else knows those secret conversations that are privy only to you and your Maker. Can you lie to yourself? Yes, you can; but you would know. Will you lie about yourself? There is no reason to, for you still would know. Deep reflection causes you to know, it is your conscience.

The title of this book with 'Part One' unceremoniously inserted as a sub-subtitle suggests a sequel of several books covering progressive periods of my early life and times in transition, of which this book is the first. Three other books will necessarily follow to reflect upon the other stages. Each of the four stages offer different events, hence quite divergent experiences, they affect us differently not simply of themselves but also because we have changed—our motives, thinking, perceptions, and feelings—have succumbed to the fluxes and refluxes of living. It is as the Potter with clay in His hand, and through kneading 'wetted' it, distributing the water evenly into its substance. Clay varies in *elasticity* or malleability, *porosity* or water absorption, and *shrinkage* in size when water is removed. We are just like that clay. Our Potter is truly the Master, with perfect skills to understand the nature of the clay. He is skilful at *centring* the clay by pressing downward and inward to obtain rotational symmetry, to *opening* the centred hollow, *flooring* the flat and rounded bottom, *throwing/pulling* to draw up and shape the wall to secure uniform thickness, *trimming/turning* to remove excess clay and refine the shape.

This book and the others to follow, I pray, will move us from enjoying the individual *events* of life, and through diligent reflection to wholly understanding a *concept* of life: from the 'little' bundle of big things to the 'big bundle' of little things.

HOW THIS BOOK IS ORGANISED

———◆⬦◆———

Every chapter will appear in three parts: the *event, additional information* about the event, and *reflection* on the event.

A narrative of the particular **event** presented as it happened from the way I saw and remembered it at that time. Each event is a chronological recollection, in narrative form, like reporting in 'black and white', with no embellishments or varnish or shades. The idea is to pass it on as experienced then. There have been instances where an event meant a general collective of similar happening that recurred throughout that period of my life and hence warranted just one general reporting. It could also be about a person or persons who prevailed throughout the book.

Following each event is a section of **additional information** to throw further light on the event. These may be from a time before the event or from a time long after the event. I came to know them from direct and/or indirect sources. They change nothing of the event but serve only to clarify or expose the reporting of it.

Next is a section of **reflection** of what I had made of it now or for some time before now. Such insight intends to be meditative and expository in nature as it reveals lessons for me that I wish to pass on to you the reader. The chapters generally end with questions and musings further elucidated or expanded in the **Endnotes** at the end of each chapter.

PROLOGUE

To every thing there is a season, and a time
to every purpose under the heaven:
A time to be born, and a time to die; a time to plant,
and a time to pluck up that which is planted;
A time to kill, and a time to heal; a time to
break down, and a time to build up;
A time to weep, and a time to laugh; a time
to mourn, and a time to dance;
A time to cast away stones, and a time to gather stones together;
a time to embrace, and a time to refrain from embracing;
A time to get, and a time to lose; a time to
keep, and a time to cast away;
A time to rend, and a time to sew; a time to
keep silence, and a time to speak;
A time to love, and a time to hate; a time
of war, and a time of peace.
What profit hath he that worketh in that wherein he laboureth?
I have seen the travail, which God hath given
to the sons of men to be exercised in it.
—King Solomon in Ecclesiastes 3

*I*nnocence . . . . is about a short memory of experiences, blended with ignorance of the unknown, exposure to a limited range of experiences, that brings on an intrepid bravado, a stance of unquenchable optimism. Things happened, and one responds to or rises to meet the occasions as they happened. At the age of *innocence,* responses are *instinctive*, innate, spontaneous; less *intuitive*, less considered, less deliberate.

That is not a definition but a recapitulation of reflections I make of my experiences in events from about age 3 to 12. *Why that age range?* That is my sense of the observable logical break in the flow of my life that is a function of the 'system' that I was born into: the small island state of Singapore, in physical and geographical terms, the social milieu, the historical, and cultural settings, the economic and political conditions. They were set in the context of that time and age, as to when one enters school, and the time one can normatively expect to leave the *education* system to enter the next. One knows when one can expect to enter the *economic* work system and become a measurable productive unit of it, statistically when to marry/wed and raise a family, with its contingent compelling considerations for housing, family size, and the maintenance of a desired lifestyle in the *social* system. The end of an economically active life decides when we retire and how we retire. Life made sense when it fitted in with the environment, such that we were round pegs in round holes or square pegs in square holes. Is life not unlike a blueprint conceptualised by our birth settings, partly endowed, partly designed by rulers of our society, through a vision/dream of sorts that can be caused only by specific policies and their attainments? *Are we a product of circumstances and/or the physical-cultural-political-socio-economic environment?*

The events are my memory and offer a travel in time, a travel in my early history. They are for learning, as much about learning, and about discovery. I have come to realise my cup of reflections is not full and writing this book had helped to fill it up a little, there is still more to uncover and discover. As I learn, am transformed, I feel the need to share. Perhaps, the *age of innocence* never ever leaves us until we draw our last breath, for it provides the basis on which we build the other *ages* of our lives. Its memories and reflections I must write about and share.

I dare not presume that all have cherished their age of innocence. We each have it differently, for one it might have been the spark of a pattern set to replicate, or pursued for much of life, for another it was best 'forgotten' though not erased, for still another it carried no deep-seated unction and soon dissipated formlessly, and assimilated nebulously without trace into one's existence.

Endnotes

Forgive me for an endnote in the Prologue, rather unusual, out-of-place. It is necessary in order that I do not clutter the main with the 'asides'. Yet, the asides illuminate the centre of what this book is. There may be moments when the writing strays from the centre, and you the reader would recall this endnote.

We are rooted to nature. A seed cannot grow into something of its own kind; it must first die to itself. The seed when planted in the ground and in cooperation with nature—its elements—changes into something significantly different from the little seed that it was. It is as the caterpillar feeds voraciously, then spins a cocoon (chrysalis) about itself, goes into an inactive non-feeding stage, and in due time breaks out with wings as a butterfly. The caterpillar dies to itself when it becomes a pupa, which then dies to it to become a butterfly.

The system we are born into is perhaps the *penultimate* cause and possibly one of several secondary causes. That begs the existence of an *ultimate* cause. To everything, there is a season, and a time to every purpose under the heaven. To every human situation, there are the extremes and we can expect to experience them, is it then a wonder at all of the human condition?

As nature goes through its paces in time and season, so do we humans go through our stages of life? What might these be? We have but two lives, not stages: the natural man that we all are, and the spiritual man, only when we have God's spirit in us. The former is the *old* man and the latter the *new* man: the *carnal* man and the *spiritual* man. The seed of God is in man for God created man. Man had separated from God when he was disobedient to His command. Man is in darkness that he cannot perceive the God of Light. Man must die to his carnal self and let the Spirit of God rouse him to a desire for reconciliation with God. God draws him, awakes him as to his dreadfully sinful nature, causes him to regenerate, to realise his own dark nature, to repent of it and turn to God for help and forgiveness. He shall come forth as that newly born butterfly.

God is the *primary* cause of all that happens in the universe; nothing has intrinsic power to cause. God in all His wisdom has also allowed for *secondary* causes. We can rightly say that God (primary cause) sends the storm wreaking much damage, yet the storm can be said to be caused by a changing winds to redirect a typhoon to make landfall (secondary cause). Meteorologists, geographers, and scientists study the phenomenon to understand and further explain the cause and effect of processes behind it. What caused the typhoon, why the landfall? Many phenomena that God created have been subjects of study by scientists to seek better understanding. They are just beginning to unravel the mysteries of God's almighty hands at work, but only barely scraping the surface.

Family photo—4 children in 1957: oldest sister Yu standing at front row far left; second sister Zhu standing at front row far right; Pa standing at middle of back row carrying me, with Mie on his left, brother Cai still a baby then sitting on grandma's lap; GGA (great grand aunt) is seated next to Zhu.

Family photo—8 children by 1964: moving clockwise from Yu seated on arm of chair at far right, down to Lian seated on floor, Zuan, I behind Zuan, Cai, Sun, Zhu on the floor far left, Mie seated on a stool carrying Zhen, Pa standing at back row far left. Grandma seated on Mie's left.

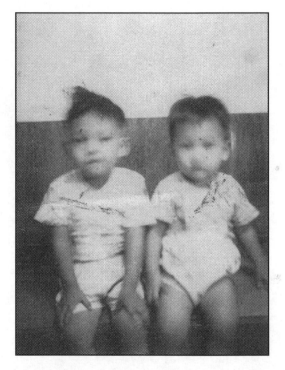

Photo of me at circa age 3,
with Cai my younger brother, on my left.

1

Baby Brother Given Away

I was three years old, seated with my back against the wall, on the single bed along the length of our bedroom? Mie handed me a baby all wrapped up in white. I saw only the head, and the hands were wrapped in and around with a white cloth. Mie helped me with my left hand to hold up the baby, and with my right to touch it. She very gently smiled and asked that I carry my little brother. I remembered my delight and began to stroke his left cheek, touched his dark thick chock of hair. I spoke to my baby brother with the little range of vocabulary I carried at that age.

A few moments later, Mie touched my shoulders drawing my attention to her and said with firmness and gentleness, "little brother will go away to stay and live with someone else. You will not see him again. Now, give him a kiss and say goodbye."

I remonstrated, and cried. Mie, holding back her tears, gently removed little brother from my hold, leaving her friend to placate me. I scrambled out of the bed and ran out to the living room with Mie's friend restraining me. I saw Mie handing little brother over to a neatly dressed woman with a tall man next to her. She held baby brother smiling broadly, said a few words to Mie and they left quickly without fuss.

Years later, while we were house cleaning, we came across the Petition for Adoption certificate issued by the Court and Pa explained the event above. My little brother was the sixth child (would be the third boy, I was the third child and the oldest boy) in our family. The adopting couple had been childless, the husband was a manager with Fraser & Neave, an established business organization, and Mie knew the couple somewhat through a close neighbour friend.

Mie had not been in the best of health before and after little brother's birth. Pa works as a daily-rated fitter, a sort of handy man, with the PWD (Public Works Department) and our livelihood was a struggling one. Having another little one to care for at that time was physically demanding on Mie and financially strenuous on Pa.

When Mie let me handle Baby Brother for the first and last time, I can now feel a sickly unexplainable sentiment—of having someone and almost immediately of losing him—like an unkindly joke. What was the purpose? At the same time, perhaps I was the oldest boy in the family the knowledge of the adoption was something to pass on to me.

Baby brother's departure pre-planned some while before, with the information that a baby boy would become available by a certain time and as word went about, the adopting party came forward for discussions. The adoption became a reality soon after his delivery, Pa and Mie arranged for sending him away. I cannot recall of having formed any meaningful attachment to him before the event above.

Under the circumstances we were in, Pa and Mie must have talked this over for months leading up to the event. They had to have the resolve to be strong, pragmatic, and thoughtful about giving away one's own flesh and blood. The hurt to them as parents to have little brother adopted out must have been painful and heart wrenching, deep beyond understanding, and always remained unfathomable to me. The situation then was hopeless. In those days, the attitude was that '*man proposes; heaven disposes*'; all was fated to be, simply destiny.

For sure and to our comfort, little brother did not move away to a place lesser than or equal to ours. The adopting parents were respectable and able people with means; they were simply childless. They would love him as their own. He was a boy and in the Chinese tradition a welcome joy.

Mie recovered from poor health and went on to add another two girls and a boy to the family. A large family of children where each child a year apart, filled the air with their voices, immensely energetic at their incessant activity that made light of dim and meagre circumstances; it was ever a surprising joy. Each child had a personality, the older cared for the younger, and the younger looked up to the older; there was *unquestionable willingness to huddle, and be in a fellowship of bonds, and of kinship,* as little pieces of charcoal placed closely together keeping each other aglow to produce a concerted heat to warm each other and all around.

This event, the first one that I recollected, was impressionable. It was my first memory of being in the world. It was the first that I had of a loved one taken from me. Perhaps, a kinder way to look at it is that we gave away a loved one, of kinship, to another outside of kinship, who would love and shower him with blessings that we were unable to vouchsafe.

Almost two decades later, even though we knew where baby brother was, through his adopted name indicated in the Adoption Petition, we made a cursory acquaintance without further pursuit. Not everyone had a connection with him other than a sentimental meaning of kinship, of flesh and blood; no one had a deep sense of loss over it. For me it was at the juncture when I could barely make any sense of a relationship with him, and the immediate detachment from him left no appendages of memory. At the time of adoption, the decision was made, with no intent to break it. That stays, it was an agreement witnessed before the courts between the natural parents of the adopted and the legal parents of the adopted.

When the loss has little nurtured or accumulated emotional attachment, letting it go can seem easy. There is little fight to resist the loss. Little brother adopted out at birth with hardly any time or opportunity for him and for us to nurture or accumulate an emotional relationship was precisely that.

A time to get, and a time to lose; a time to keep, and a time to cast away.

Endnotes

Before Mie and Pa found God in their later years, the philosophy of life was about fate, an unknown heaven, an unknown and unknowable Supreme Being. Once God came into their hearts, they saw God's mercy that binds and *breaks not the bruised reed*, as the Hope that fans and *quenches not the smoking flax*. We were the bruised reeds who by His grace lifted us out of the seeming despair. In His merciful providence, He offers the joy of healing. When He takes away, He gives to overflowing! Remember, our God is the Lord of life.

He heals the broken in heart, and binds up their wounds.

2

Firecrackers

It was Chinese New Year day and Pa carried me in the crook of his left hand, went out of the house and with his right he lighted a large red fire cracker with a smoking cigar. The fuse burned, got shorter, and Pa threw it up into the air so I could see the cracker explode in mid air. I found this all very fascinating. He threw a few more and let me down. We went into the house and the adults went on talking among themselves.

I edged myself towards the coffee table, picked out a similar large firecracker, and found a smoking cigar that rested on an ashtray at the corner coffee table. I did exactly what I saw earlier and could see the fuse sizzling away and then there was the explosion. Everybody turned about to see what caused it. In a delayed shock, I cried out in pain as my index finger bled . . .

A cracker is like a mini-dynamite stick filled with gunpowder that explodes when the fuse is lighted up. A grand uncle from Penang had visited and he smoked nothing but cigars. I was a curious four-year old and did not know how to hold a firecracker. I held it near its middle, the way I would grab most things within my reach. That was where the cracker let go its 'bang'. My right index finger bled about the middle phalange. The injury was bad and the scar stayed with me for life, though not as visibly now to someone unaware of this event.

———⟨≫⟩———

Our lives were full of experiments at ages three and four. The experiment led to an unforgettable *physical* experience and I do not really remember any great trauma resulting from it. The pain was gone *quickly* and I understood pain as bearable. Through much of my life, pain, be it physical, psychological, or emotional, despite being hurtful is acceptably *bearable and manageable*. After this incident, at every Chinese New Year, I discovered many new progressive ways of handling the large firecracker, even to the point of holding it between my fingers without getting hurt as it exploded. As with the way experiments were designed—with studied caution—the first attempt begun with slipping the cracker through a hole in a piece of paper, which served as a 'guard' against the explosion. The ultimate was to hold the cracker as it exploded, without getting hurt.

As I grew up, I attempted many *experiments*. They showed the better way forward, and rewarded me with priceless experiences. Strangely, at no price at all! If there was one, it was too small to keep me away from my love for experimentation. In these experiments, miniature *decisions and judgments* made were with the intent only to satisfy the momentary whims and fancies of a young child. The impact of failures was too limited to sink the spirit of a child, and the ecstasy of successes too explosively short, enough only to carry him over into the next experiment.

Experiments are attempts at pushing the limits, in time or space. With every attempt, more is learned, difficulties overcome, and the bar rose. It is all a virtuous cycle. There is cause and effect. There is responsibility and consequence. Execution of the former determines outcomes of the latter.

Little pains, troubles, afflictions are life's way of preparing us for the road ahead. The cup of affliction is one we must all drink. With the experiences, we can, with confidence and in faith, deal with more and greater pains, trials, and difficulties. These may not just be physical in nature but very often, they stretch us emotionally. They exercise our potential, enlarge the boundaries of our understanding, and grant us strength.

One very distinctive observation about this event was that when Pa burnt that first firecracker, my young mind was attentive to the *process* of firing off the firecracker and not bothered at all about the *outcome*. My excitement was to know how to work the process, the outcome was a 'given'. Experiments are much like that, deep interest in how to better the way that made things work, and work better. Experiments are inquiries into how things work and why they are. Inherent in them is cause and effect. Is it not for the purpose, the outcome, the theory, or hypothesis that we want to prove when we perform experiments?

Endnotes

What is beyond the earthly life? Who proffers us direction, extends wise counsels, and prepares us for the journey? It would be without profit if all that we live for comes to nothing but dust that cannot even see or experience the dreams and hopes we hold while living. To be at all profitable, dreams and hopes must consummate in our Creator.

What is faith? "Now faith is the substance of things hoped for, the evidence of things not seen." Faith does not count on feeling, is indifferent to emotion, disinterested in circumstances, unconcerned with the self-evident. Faith looks with fearful trust in God's merciful love, in His *promise* of the glorious hope in an eternal life, on the condition of belief in His Son Jesus Christ; whose death on the cross was the efficacious propitiation for our sins, while we, in our depravity are unable to secure satisfaction to meet the demands of His covenant. All who do not believe Him shall be condemned to everlasting darkness. Faith rests on God's demonstrated love, mercy, and grace; not on a fuzzy, nice, warm, tender feeling. It is a fidelity to God, a reliance on Him, a trust in Him.

What is our potential? Where are its borders? To don the character of Christ and of God is our purpose; we are but worms on the extreme opposite pole. That huge gulf is our potential. Yield to the Spirit, work out our salvation. The Word of God is the only hedge, Christ your only hope.

3

Washing in exchange for lesson

I Remembered Mie took me to a flat in the adjacent block. She introduced me to the mistress of the flat who was about Mie's age. Mie introduced me as her son and that I would learn English from her. She took a printed book and asked me whether I knew the alphabet, to which I moved my head from left to right, signalling that I knew it not. We proceeded with the lesson. She had a long wooden table with several other children, students rather, seated at it in an orderly manner. She asked me to sit at the most corner one.

Mie had proceeded to the kitchen and bathroom area away from the living hall where we were. She seemed to know the place well. I was familiar with the layout as it was identical to our flat in the adjacent block.

After about an hour, Mie re-appeared and thanked the teacher. Mie said something to her about the clothes she had put out to dry on bamboo poles. On the way home, Mie enquired about my lesson for that morning. I learnt about alphabets: twenty-six in all. I knew how to read and write the first one—the big 'A' and the small 'a'.

———— ❖ ————

In those days there were no washing machines, the laundry was hand washed and a saw-teeth or jagged surface scrub-board against which to scrub the clothes. That can be hard on gentle hands but Mie was used to this. When Mie was at home, she washed certain clothes and starched them before putting out to dry. After drying, she would spray water to soften them for ironing, much like what grandpa did at the Tiong Bahru kampong.

Mie told me the washing paid for the lesson I received that day. It had all been agreed and pre-arranged. Apparently, the washing had more value than the lesson so Mie was able to keep some takings. Mie and I went back there every Monday, Wednesday, and Friday. I cannot recall when it was that this whole episode of washing-in-exchange-for-lesson terminated. Probably not very long, like after six months. By then, I had completed study of two textbooks and had written on about two exercise books. Mie and Pa were overjoyed that I became strongly conversant with simple reading and able to write the alphabets and simple words, correctly spelled, by the teacher's markings.

———— ❖ ————

In looking back, I can only imagine Pa and Mie placing their hopes in their children to receive the schooling they both never had. Mie's washing-in-exchange-for-lesson taught me much about the love, hope, and joy of our parents in our lives, and the sacrifices they were willing to lay upon themselves. Mie had started me early by drawing my interest to study and learning. I went over and over the two textbooks, as I did not have anything else to read. It was an excellent early preparation for my entry to primary one; it kept any transition shock at bay.

The washing-in-exchange-for-lesson approach was a very innovative barter when one had no means of putting up the cold hard cash. From it, I had learnt negotiation, win-win, trade-ins and trade-offs. These concepts, and their principles were applied subconsciously early in life and through my working life.

Children must cherish our parents' love and hope. They encouraged and celebrated our achievements; encouraged and consoled us when the chips were down. They were anxious when we failed in health, when we returned home late from school or on a night out, when examinations were just around the corner, when we met a new girl, and when our pockets were dry. Do not grieve them. Love them by our obedience and devotion. Above all, honour them with our 'fruits' so that they are respected by others.

I often recall the love of Pa and Mie in providing for our needs and development in seemingly untenable conditions. *Early education gave us a head start* and put us on the track that mattered much in our upbringing.

Give her of the fruit of her hands; and let her own works praise her in the gates.

LOVE always finds the best available Means . . . God in His providence gave the means.

Schooling, our son must have,
Much hope we have in him.
Money, we have not,
Still schooling, he must have.
By labours of washing,
Schooling, our son shall have.

4

Zhu, my second sister

Second sister whose name was Bao Zhu (meaning 'precious pearl') was one year older than I. One day, she saw me writing my homework assigned by the washing-in-exchange-for-lesson teacher and wanted to do the same. I gave her a piece of paper and copied out three alphabets A, B, C, for her to follow. We never treated Zhu as retarded in speech. Within the home, we could communicate with her, and she with us. She did most of the things we did, we played together, and we ate together, she fended for us when Mie wanted to cane us for disobedience . . . . Pa and Mie never enrolled Zhu for school.

She did not hold the pencil in the correct way. Her written 'A' was disproportionately short and wide, the two legs were of unequal lengths. Her writing of 'B' and 'C' were inversed as in a mirror image. She never quite pronounced them. She wanted to write whenever we were at it. She wanted to be in on the activity and it became a fun thing for her.

Mie was pregnant with Zhu when she slipped and fell at the market. She recovered and did not think too much about the incident. It was some years after Zhu was born, that Pa and Mie realised she was mentally retarded. Zhu's birthday fell on 1st April 1954.

We dearly loved Zhu. We protected her much from the outside world. There was a stigma about *mental retardation* in those days. Perhaps it was by design that the thoughtless neighbourhood kids called her 'dumb', for Choo had been unable to communicate beyond just some sounds and squawks. At some point, the word 'mad' rolled off the tongues of those outside of our home, thoughtless, and hurtful as it may seem.

Just as an aside, our Chinese names carry auspicious meanings. Unlike the Western nomenclature, our names begin with a SURNAME followed by a MIDDLE_NAME and an END_NAME. Mine is like HE TIAN FU. The surname was the family name.

I will list below, my siblings by their gender in order of age, oldest first. All the girls carry a middle name 'Bao' meaning precious. All the boys have for their middle name 'Tian' meaning add or increase.

Girls: Yu (jade, she was oldest sister), Zhu (pearl, was second sister), Lian (chain), Zuan (diamond), and Zhen (value).

Boys: Fu (happiness/blessedness), Cai (wealth), Chen (success, of course he was my little brother who was adopted out), and Sun (smoothness as in flow, without heckles).

———————⟨≫⟩———————

Life in our strata of society at that time was one of 'live and let live'. There was a sense of fatalism about it. Today, when a pregnant woman has a fall, she would go see a gynaecologist—a specialist doctor—to make sure the baby is well. Access to good medical services is common these days, and people are cautious and better educated. Medical services were not so accessible then. There was only one GP clinic in the locality where we lived and it opened on certain days. The consultation fee was often several times that of the one and only government outpatient clinic that opened for six days a week. This government clinic was always crowded because the fees were heavily subsidised by the state. However, we had to collect a queue ticket at 7.30 in the morning. We never could afford use of the GP clinic. As how society was organised: government clinics were for the masses, while private clinics for the select rich. We all grew up generally very healthy with rare visits to the doctor. We had one cure for all ailments: fever tablets, much like paracetamol today, with lots of water and sleep. Once in all while Pa used 'kan mao cha', a traditional Chinese tea that was highly effective in causing our bodies to sweat out the cold or flu. This was definitely a proven cure for me when the cold was stubborn and fever was at the door.

Having a second sister such as Zhu was a gift, a blessing of sorts. She may not have the full faculties of a normal person but she had a big heart, call it love, for her siblings. *Life is not always in the head, it is really a lot of the heart.* Her place in our lives had taught us patience, love, and just letting her being herself. Yes, she loved freedom. She made us laugh often when she got her written alphabets looking weird or tried to sing. She would sing for long when in the mood, it was unintelligible, simply sounds within a narrow range of intonations. She had been for us a bundle of joy, pain, anxiety, and surprisingly pleasant experiences. She revealed a zeal for life that easily exceeded what any of us had, if not constrained by her faculties. *What a giant example!*

Zhu had significantly influenced me in the way I think about life, the purposes that physical and intelligent endowments serve, whether normal or irregular. I thought a lot about how she might live out her life with us as it was, and she would be fine. Her life had its stages too; unlike how I thought, that it could juxtapose ours. We force-fitted her life into ours, and accommodated whenever possible. That was not how reality worked out.

Endnotes

Zhu was God-sent. The effect on me was indelible, when I carried Zhu from the taxi the day she got home with Mie from Woodbridge Hospital when I was fifteen. Emaciated, her frame was simply bones wrapped loosely in a thin layer of unwilling skin that had lost its elasticity; the life and energy in better times drained off by her dying body. In the space of a short time, everything changed . . . completely confounded by the devastating circumstances, the utter unfairness, and the lack of purpose if there was one. The better times we had before were in one heavy sweep hitched to a millstone and cast into the deeps, our voiceless sorrow overwhelming, and our hearts full and brimming with unutterable pain. Clock time stopped; her physical presence with it. I entered another kind of time altogether. Zhu's lingering presence pressed on and never really left us. We will hear more of her is in my next book.

Mental retardation in those days focused on cognition, on knowledge, on perception, but known now to include mental functioning and the individual's functional skills in the environment. As a result, a person with a below-average intelligence quotient (IQ) is not necessarily mentally retarded. Experience and research today had grown the body of knowledge in science and medicine that could benefit Zhu in her times. Woodbridge would not be merely a mental hospital where anything concerning deficiencies of the mind is tagged 'Woodbridge' a sad connotation of 'madness'. We must be grateful that we have today an Institute of Mental Health, a friendlier name with a better understanding of mental retardation and hence a more precise segmentation and classification of the nuances of a condition for application of the appropriate treatment.

Wedding Picture of Pa and Mie

5

Pa, my father

P a was with me in a bus on our way home. I was tired and the rocking of the bus lulled me to sleep. He carried me with my head over his shoulder and walked home from the bus stop. Along the way, I was out of my sleep but decided to keep my eyes opened without any sign of having woken up. It was a real treat to for a strong Pa to carry me, all secured and cosy. He also carried my younger brother when I was able to walk strongly on my own. Physically, Pa never tired.

———◈———

Pa was Fujian (a southern province in China), was not very tall unlike his oldest brother. Pa had a tanned look while uncle was fair. Both wore spectacles. Pa's youngest brother was shorter. It seemed like height went with age. Often, when the three brothers were in a discussion on issues of life, Pa seemed to take the lead, but he listened when the subject changed to uncles' office work, financial and industry matters.

Pa featured as someone who had done rough work, skinny, and strong but not brawny. Pa worked as a fitter and spent much time in the sun at the different work sites all over Singapore whenever there was a problem with manhole chokes or pump failures. Pa was very much like a trouble-shooter, always fixing problems that were pump related. He was quick-tempered and ever ready to set right any wrong that he perceived to be, through which one could see his kindness and fairness as a person. Pa arrived in Singapore in 1948 after the end of the War. He sailed from Penang with a ship and served as a coolie to load and unload sacks of rice. He was 23 years of age when he landed in Singapore and found regular work before marrying Mie a few years later.

Pa's family was from Phuket Island on the west side of the Kra Isthmus which joined Thailand (then known as Siam) and Malaysia (then known as Malaya). Pa's grandpa was an admiral in the Thai Navy. The family was wealthy, owned several houses, and operated tin mines. Phuket used to flourish in the tin mining industry. Pa told us that he had several uncles who were simply lazy, womanised, and smoked opium. They did not maintain the family business in good order but instead squandered the family's wealth with nothing left to posterity.

Pa was a Phuket Baba Chinese or Peranakan and had kinship ties to the Straits Settlement Babas through the Penang Babas. Grandpa was Phuket Baba and married grandma who was Penang Baba. Babas were Chinese men who came mostly from Fujian in southern China. They married women from Malaya and developed a hybrid culture that mixed local practices and colonial values, but kept the Chinese identity. Grandma was a nonya, a woman Baba.

———❖———

Pa provided what he was able to from his lack of schooling and financial limitation, and I as son brought him help in overcoming his illiteracy along the way. Pa had an old ancient-looking red English-Thai dictionary that was thick pocket-sized and cloth-bound. The covers were coming off and the pages yellowed badly with the edges browned, Pa had taped the backbone and covers securely. It helped him pick up English sufficiently to be able to pronounce or read simple passages. By an iterative process, he would ask me about a word and I would pronounce it for him, he would try it, looked up the English-Thai dictionary, and compared my explanation. Later on, when Mie started her 'amah' career and worked for British military families, Pa had opportunities to progress in stammering English as he tried to converse with them. I became the default family reader and writer as Pa would have me study or explain documents he received in the mail or from work.

More importantly, our academic achievements at school brought upon him praises from all around. Pa claimed no credit of his own as he considered himself unschooled. It was encouraging for Pa as he appreciated the value of a good education even more. We always had a reverential and filial love for Pa. In our younger days, we carried some unknown fear of him but over time, as we understood how Pa operated, and he begun to shed some of his 'cold-tough' front, that fear shifted to love. I always felt secured with Pa as he was strong, straight talking and transparent. It was always black or white, and no shades of grey. Pa was seldom diplomatic whenever he sensed a bad idea or thought.

Pa was a good problem solver with mechanical hardware. I had seen him discussing matters of life, and he was able to similarly deal with those situations.

We are alike, in whatever station in life. We are born and we die. That is our beginning and our end. How we live between birth and death, between the beginning and end, makes a difference. *When blessed with great fathers we find blessed children who in turn have the potential to make great fathers.*

He becomes poor that deals with a slack hand: but the hand of the diligent makes rich.

Endnotes

Even Pa's own mother considered him downtrodden, unable to rise above the dregs of society. Our God raised him to honour, took him into the fold, sent manna sufficient for the day, showered him with nine children, and cast on him innumerable joys. Our God loves all alike. We are all 'worms', downright nothing and yet His smile is upon us; He hears every flutter, every palpitation, every throb, every desire of our heart. His hand is never too short that He cannot save, nor his hearing too hard that He cannot hear.

The LORD preserveth the simple: I was brought low, and he helped me.

A *good* name *is* rather to be chosen than great riches, *and* loving favour rather than silver and gold. The rich and poor meet together: the LORD *is* the maker of them all.

Later photo of Mie—notice the hairdo, very common and popular in the 'go-go' era, age of the Beatles. Mie had it done to attend someone's wedding.

6

Mie, my mother

We addressed Mie as short for Mummie. Mie was slim, generally soft spoken, also of few words, gentle, not convincingly pretty, always neatly attired, and ready to extend a helping hand and act upon a moment's call. She was endlessly busy: marketing some, sweeping, wiping or washing, and of course minding the children. We were quite a handful.

She was a submissive wife to Pa. Mie was born and bred in Singapore. She was Cantonese (a dialect group) and ten years younger than Pa. Mie spoke more Fujian than Cantonese because when young, her father sent her to live and work with a Fujian family. Her mother had died when she was young.

Like Pa, Mie did not receive formal schooling, and could not write, nor read. Later on, Mie began to write her name and alias in English, that is, only the alphabets that spelt her name; anything more than those alphabets, she was at a loss. You may tag her 'a copy-er'. Yes, her identified name was the Cantonese name, and the alias was the Fujian name. She even learnt to write her Cantonese name in Chinese as a 'copy-er'. Mie also learnt to write one to ten in Chinese. Some years later, she was able to pick up enough key English words to send her to work as amah for several British military families stationed in Singapore. When the British troops returned home, Mie had a break and went to work as amah for an American oil executive.

She was quite a 'toughie', emotionally sensitive and meek; very rarely, when pushed to the edge, would she throw up a startling retort. I have seen her feeling hurt and disappointed over something Pa said that had been insensitive, or some unkind words from grandma, when she would turn away to quietly sob in private. Endurance supplanted retaliation. There was no sense of stoicism; it was more a case of accepting and working with the circumstances knowing she had no control over them. To sum up, she carried about her a quiet fortitude that faced all events and outcomes bravely, cheerfully, and patiently.

The Chinese zodiac had twelve animals that represented the lunar calendar year in which one was born. Mie was born under the 'pig' sign. We often joked that it fitted her perfectly as she had given birth to nine children! That was the full string and quite a marvel. In those days having many children was simply commonplace.

Mie had no religion; she tagged along with Pa to the Thai temple on special occasions or events but had no devotion to it at all other times. She did the necessary that would keep Pa or anyone out of embarrassment.

Mie knew her place in life, accepted her portion as a wife who submitted to her husband: loyal to his leading, willingly endure the unpleasant and difficult, never displaying evidence of complaint. As mother, she cared for and attended to the development of her children. Not that she had any skills in teaching or the 3Rs (reading, writing, and arithmetic). What she had about her was this *sense of*

principle and integrity that manifested itself in whatever she said or did. It was not a character born of fortuity but one beaten against the hard inhospitable surface of reality in society. The fruits of endurance and strength had found their way into her frame, of body and of mind.

However, because we lived with grandma, Mie had to take a great deal of heartless, uncharitable, mean, thoughtless, spiteful remarks from her.

Endnotes

Mie although quiet was friendly, ever thoughtful, courteous, and sensible. She was dedicated and self-denying. However, very importantly, Mie was astute, scrupulous, sincere, and rational. In the labyrinth of life, there was little room for miscalculation: survival, at the 'moment of truth' and sustenance, for the longer. In her case, simplicity ruled.

Who can find a virtuous woman? For her price is far above rubies.
The heart of her husband doth safely trust in her, so that he shall have no need of spoil.
She will do him good and not evil all the days of her life.
She seeks wool, and flax, and worketh willingly with her hands.

Strength and honour are her clothing; and she shall rejoice in time to come.
She opens her mouth with wisdom; and in her tongue is the law of kindness.
She looks well to the ways of her household, and eats not the bread of idleness.
Her children arise up, and call her blessed; her husband also, and he praises her.
Many daughters have done virtuously, but you excel them all.

Traditional wedding photo of grandpa and grandma, notice the
Peranakan dressing with significant traces of Chinese elements
in the long dress, the ornamental chains about the neck, the
wrist bangles, and the Baba traces in the headdress and shoes.
I have no idea whether this was a real location or a studio
shot, notice the floor tiles, and the window design.

7

Grandma

This chapter might have read Grandpa and Grandma. However, grandpa died at the age of twenty-nine. Pa was only very little then, under five years. Grandma was a nonya, a Straits Settlement Chinese, or Peranakan woman from Penang somewhere up to the north-west of the Malayan peninsula. She wears a sarong from the waist down like an open-bottom sack wrapped around the body, held about the waist by a silver girdle, a silver metal belt made with many interlinked buckles.

She had a tendency to make comments about practically everything and anything, almost a non-stop mouth that uttered what was on her mind, and those thoughts were often not pretty. A lot like gossiping, complaining, and talking bad about someone, and the like. She would almost constantly chew a kind of leaf in which she had wrapped some ingredients. I think she called it 'sireh', a Malay or Straits Settlement or Penang word for the betel leaf. I later learned that it wrapped the areca nut and lime for chewing, and when she spitted out it was all red like blood. I never understood how she could chew the sireh and talked simultaneously. In that very act alone, I perceived the image of a 'busy-body'.

I never liked grandma. She had the habit of grabbing me towards her and kissing me on the cheek. Yuck!

⊰⊱

Grandma spoke the Fujian dialect sprinkled with Malay, very typical of Babas (the males) and Nonyas (the females). I must have picked up Malay from all the conversations. Grandma was the matriarch of the family, as grandpa passed away at an early age of 29 from tuberculosis. No one seemed to know anything about grandpa except grandma. Grandma remarried to a Eurasian, decades later before any of us children were born, and became a nominal Roman Catholic because of her new husband.

Grandma was simply a tyrant and came across as someone who always wanted to receive a benefit but not one willing to give any. Pa was the second son, my first uncle was an accountant at Harpers Gilfillan, and my youngest uncle was a bank officer at the Mercantile Bank. In short, my Pa and all of us lived with grandma because Pa could ill afford to have his own house. My two uncles have their own terraced houses in the Serangoon Garden area. They gave grandma a monthly allowance to take care of the flat rental and maintenance, as well as living expenses. I also believe that conventionally, one son, meaning Pa by default, stayed with grandma to take care of her. Pa and grandma never got along well as grandma never cared for Pa since young. She also had nothing good to say about Pa, often insinuating the differences between Pa and her other two sons that essentially hinged on the matter of money. Pa had no education and had to fend for himself at a very young age. There was just a huge gulf between son and mother, which seemed irreconcilable. They hardly talked to each other with observable disdain of each other.

In later years, when grandma was down with diabetes, their difficult relationship softened somewhat, perhaps from dad's sympathy, maturity, and the close kinship between them. Mercy covered over the old and passionate hatreds. Wrongs, all have committed. Errors all have crossed. *To err is human; to forgive is divine*.

Love of family members for each other does not just happen, it requires tending, nurturing. Even though the gulf between Pa and Grandma was so unbridgeable, Pa attached deference to Grandma as the woman who gave birth to him—*a sad relationship where no recognition of son-ship or motherhood existed between them but for flesh and blood.*

Endnotes

Respect for grandma prevailed in spite of her differences with Pa. Pa had always instructed us so to be. Selfishness, pride, and fear destroy sweet relationships, even of kinship. Pa and Mie reminded us of the kinship and that we cherish it with love that guards against selfishness, and fear.

Readers interested in the background of Babas in the Straits Settlements may read, Derek Heng and Syed Muhd Khairudin Ajunied (eds), *Reframing Singapore, Memory—Identity—Trans-regionalism,* ICAS/Amsterdam University Press, 2009.

For the social aspects of the betel leaf chewing practice, readers may refer to, Chan Kwok Bun and Tong Chee Kiong (eds), *Past Times: A social history of Singapore*, Times Editions/Times Media Private Limited, 2003.

8

Indian jamu

I Accompanied my great grand aunt (let us shorten it to GGA) to her workplace along River Valley Road. The owner was a wealthy Indian family and the house from the outside looked like a 2-storey building until I went in on the second floor, when I realised there was a grand staircase running up to a third storey. The hallway was large, the ceilings were high, and its sheer size was awesome. There was a handful of beautiful furniture exposed and the rest draped over. Large chilli red square tiles edged with intricate gold designs covered the walls so that they looked sprightly monotonous.

A plump old woman in Indian dressing walked in from a room in the back of the house. She looked at me and beckoned me to follow her as she went over to a cabinet and took out a jar bottle, unscrewed the cap and took out two round objects with a fork and placed them in a little plate. She gave it to me signalling me to take and eat. They were light brown and 'wet', and looked like they were soaked in some liquid in the bottle. I cut up a ball with the fork and took one half. It was sweet and soft. It was nice and I liked it. The woman looked at me with delight. She seemed to know what pleased a child.

———⬦———

GGA was old, in her early seventies, and was bow-legged . . . and widowed for many decades. I accompanied her this time as she had just recovered from a bad common cold. She had worked with this Indian family for many a long years and was trusted of them. GGA was like a general household helper, from washing clothes, cleaning house, to cooking. In her earlier years, she lived in at the house. However, as her duties had lightened she lived with us at that time of this event.

Thirty years later, I learnt that the light brown food given me was *jamu*, made very simply of flour, and lightly fried, which explains the mild crisp that made it special. It is then soaked in brown sugar solution. Wow! It was so simple and yet so delicious.

———⬦———

In our meagre circumstances, this visit to a 'grand' house was a rare treat to a real place but also one that stirred a rich vein of my imagination about palaces that I came to read of in storybooks and later to watch in movies on TV.

Wealth seemed lonely: so large and opulent an abode with so few people about. I lived in a small rented 3-bedroom SIT (Singapore Improvement Trust, the colonial housing authority, forerunner of the HDB) government flat that was crammed with three families of twelve people. We share one toilet-bathroom combo: in a word, Spartan. Of course, we had the old-fashioned metal potty, twice the height of a spittoon to serve as a quick relief should the toilet be occupied.

Except for the name, I had never forgotten the *jamu* all these decades and in the recent few years I had the opportunity to savour it again when I attended an Indian friend's celebration of his daughter's birthday. The experience was just as it was at my first taste of it. Even more recently, I attended another Indian party and realised not all *jamu* taste or look the same. The size can be observably different too.

It was like a long lost delicacy . . . Still recently, I learnt from an Indian friend that I could now buy it in a can!

We can enjoy the simple things of life, even something as simple and cheap like jamu: its savour and the associated joy I remember distinctly. The palatial dwelling loses its sheen and its allure in the associated loneliness.

Endnotes

Simplicity is singleness, unmixed, uncontaminated. For a child, that singleness is sweetness. The *jamu* met that simplicity of appreciation. It was not the colour, nor the beauty of the object. It was simply sweetness.

Four of us from L to R: Yu, Zhu, me, Cai

9

Mie feeding the four

My eldest sister, second sister, I and my younger brother were all seated in that order, on the floor, cross-legged, in an arc. Mie brought a dipped-in plate with plain rice, spread over with black sauce from the black-sauce-three-layered pork, with some pork, and fried long beans. She brought in the cane as well and laid it beside her.

This was dinner for us. It was a serious activity. Mie picked up a spoonful of rice, with a tiny piece of pork, and fed the youngest (my younger brother) first. While he was chewing, she picked another spoonful of rice and a tiny piece of pork, and fed me. She did the same for second sister and eldest sister. Next round was rice and long beans. Following that round, we had rice and pork. Dinner ended when the plate of food was finished.

She stood up and went to the kitchen to refill the plate while we sat quietly and waited for her. Mie put us through this second, also the last plate of our dinner. She then ordered us to go rinse and wipe dry our mouths, and drink the plain boiled water from a glass bottle. It had cooled down by the time we finished dinner.

I hated the skin of the pork, would eat up only the meaty part, but set the skin in the corner of my mouth until Mie went to refill the plate. I would quietly and quickly run to the window and discharge the pork skin. My siblings were cooperative and said not a word when Mie returned. Until today, I shun the pork skin.

⚜

There was not much food to put on the table for everyone to sit around and dig into. By this most practical method, Mie was able to allocate the food, enough to sustain and keep us healthy. Whatever Mie doled out to us, we were to eat without murmuring or choosing in her presence. The cane was ever at hand. No choice was the best choice. There was a certain discipline about this routine for many years in our early lives.

Foolishness is *bound in the heart of a child;* but *the rod of correction shall drive it far from him.*

Until today whenever I have a meal, my plate leaves not a grain of rice. Mie used to tell my sisters that leaving a grain on the plate would result in them having pimples and spotted faces. We lived a life-long habit of not wasting. Take what we can eat and finish. This food concept spilled into general matters such as 'try what you can finish and do well', or like 'bite off what you can chew'.

Was this a case of imposing habits to cultivate behaviours?

Cultivated habits cause the change in behaviours, and in due time cause people to subconsciously become those behaviours. They create tendencies and dispositions that can dog us for life until they become part of our persona. How powerful these silent forces are in subtly influencing our behaviours for good or for worse. How dreadful that we are unable to shake them off. Habits are acquired behaviours. Personal and social habits are but cultivated. Habits soon become customs, and practised for no rhyme or reason, just the way they have been, the way we have always done them.

10

Grandma bullies Mie

Mie was choking with tears, sobbing away incessantly in the kitchen amidst grandma's loud ranting, holding a cleaver and hitting the sharp edge on the wooden chopping board over and over in tandem with her ranting. I ran into the kitchen and stood between grandma and Mie, little as I was then. Mie continued with her choking and sobbing. It appeared safer to get her into our bedroom, which I did. She then sat on the bed and asked me to go and fetch Pa who was not at home at that time. I asked Mie to lock the door while I go look for Pa. There were a few friends of Pa in the vicinity and I took a chance on one of them who is a local and whose wife was a Thai. Pa was there and I spoke to Pa privately about going home. Pa excused himself courteously and we went home.

When Pa arrived home with me, grandma toned down. There then followed an exchange between Pa and grandma. It was not respectful, not like between a mother and son.

The bullying encounters went on for a year and eventually tailed off partly because Pa was around the house often in the evening, giving grandma few opportunities to intimidate Mie. I was on and by Mie's side whenever such bullying occurred. Grandma liked me a lot and was careful not to allow her aggression to worsen the drift between us.

Years later, grandma toned down much, not mellowed though. We were then a bigger family, circumstances had improved somewhat, and grandma indulged in my youngest brother and he became grandma's favourite. Grandma began to speak civilly to Mie.

Bullying, as I reflected, was a case of grandma being unable to domineer over Pa. She took it on Mie. As matriarch, she held an overarching rule over the household except for Pa. Neglect of her responsibility for Pa in his early years had disqualified her from holding sway over him and all that was his, particularly his family of Mie and us children, try as she would. Bullying was a transfer of that frustration or irritation. It was a great deal of habitual intimidation with no physical violence exercised.

The disharmony healed with time. *Time heals*. Age also heals, circumstance heals too but all *within Time*.

11

Bukit Ho Swee Fire

We were at home and there was a frightful knock on our door, loud and in very quick succession. Pa was at work. Grandma was in Penang. Mie hurriedly went to open the door. It was our next-door neighbour, who spoke in Cantonese. Mie thanked her and shut the door behind her. Mie told us—Yu, Zhu, Cai, Lian, and I—to get together and not to go anywhere else while she packed our clothes and essentials. She said a very big fire at Bukit Ho Swee, a kampong not too far from our house, had broken out. The wind could bring it to other kampongs adjacent to our house, and we needed to prepare for removal to a safe place.

Once Mie had packed the essentials into large cloth bundles, we all waited for the worst to happen and kept watch from the bedroom windows to catch any sign of approaching fire. We were out of sight of the fire, the skies were reddish, and billowing clouds of dark smoke appeared to move up slowly and surely. Occasionally, we would see a neighbour who returned from Bukit Ho Swee shouting out an update on the fire. The winds had not blown, yet the heat could be felt somewhat.

Kampongs were autonomous clusters of local communities where cheap wooden dwellings (with zinc or *attap* roofs; attap were long branches of the coconut palm with the leaves intact) were constructed to meet the population boom. They were mostly unauthorised and housed low-income Chinese families, and were mostly on the fringes of the central area of Singapore's administrative and commercial district. SIT (Singapore Improvement Trust) the colonial housing authority had not been able to provide alternative housing to meet the boom, and the new government's HDB replaced SIT with plans to re-house these kampongs, as they were unsightly and disorganised. They have also become fire hazards. Nearest to Bukit Ho Swee (bukit is Malay for hill, Ho is Chinese for river, and Swee in Chinese for water) were Kampong Silat to its south, Kampong Tiong Bahru to its left, and Kampong Henderson immediately to the front and west of Tiong Bahru. Our house was on opposite side of Alexandra Road that separates Tiong Bahru and Henderson. If the fire had swept through these two kampongs, we would evacuate. The inferno, yes an inferno at Bukit Ho Swee as we later learnt was Singapore's largest fire and this was in May 1961 the year before I entered school for primary education.

Mie's father, her oldest brother, and his wife stayed in Kampong Tiong Bahru, while Mie's oldest sister lived in Kampong Henderson. I remembered that we regularly visited Mie's father. The house was all wooden planks, six inches in breadth and about a third of an inch thick, set horizontally and slightly overlapping each other pointing outwards. Vertical wooden beams on the other side served as superstructure of the house that held the horizontal planks. Four steps on the side stairway in front led to the house built higher than the hard ground to compromise with the terrain's contour. As one entered the house, one side was a single charcoal stove kitchen. The other side was for drying the laundry. Inside was the living hall and grandpa's high bed took one side against the wooden planked wall. On the opposite side was the dining table, nailed together from the similar wooden planks. A round electrical light bulb hung in middle of the hall hung from the ceiling of wooden beams. When we visited in the evening, grandpa switched it on and you would notice it was dim because the bulb was of low wattage to conserve electricity. Uncle's bedroom was at the far end of the house. It had an open door covered over with a curtain from the top of the doorpost down. Overall, the house was probably about twenty feet wide and thirty feet long.

At one corner was the charcoal iron which grandpa used. I have seen him ironing the clothes. He first had to burn pieces of charcoal in a clay stove in the kitchen until they were red hot. He then broke them into smaller pieces and used the tongs put them into the charcoal iron. He next sprayed the clothes with water from a little bottle with tiny holes in the cap. When the iron was ready, grandpa put it to work and steam rose as he ironed away. There was an art to ironing. I never got any closer, as grandpa said the iron was too hot and heavy for a young one like me.

The kampong was acceptably Spartan and shared a common bathroom with a hinged swing door. Any adult taking a shower had to bring his own pail to collect water from a central water stand and carry with him to the bathroom. For toileting, in an adjacent shack, one squatted to defecate through a jagged hole in the concrete floor, to land precisely or 'off the mark' into a bucket, to be cleared the next day by sewage workers in a truck that had many compartments, each to contain a bucket full of excreta. A replacement bucket took the place of the one removed from the toilet. That was the 'night-soil' carriers.

In those days, there was a large earthen pot in the toilet to contain water with a scoop to dish the water for washing off the excreta. There was no toilet paper, just hands. Little boys would stand and urine into any makeshift drains there were, while little girls squatted over them.

Laundry washing took place at the central water stand, where several women would gather daily. They squeezed the laundry dry, brought home to air and dry out. The washers had to take turns in groups depending on the space around the water stand.

I recalled the 'kampong' or community spirit where our neighbour passed on information about the fire to Mie to prepare for possible eventuality, even while we lived in SIT flats. At Tiong Bahru kampong where we visited most often, I could see a form of self-organisation as the voluntary refilling of the earthen pot in the toilet, with water from the central water stand. As blazes were common in the kampong, they had a fire-fighting stand just outside a wooden coffee shop at the entry to the kampong. A provision store stood next to the coffee shop. The fire-fighting stand had a stack of pails painted over in red and a low wooden sand box. A hanging mid-sized bell hung next to the sand box, for use as an alarm by anyone who had first sight of or relayed knowledge of a fire.

The Bukit Ho Swee fire was the turning point in public housing. The Housing and Development Board (HDB) came into prominence and made home ownership accessible to every citizen in Singapore. They built flats on the site where the kampong razed to the ground. The public housing program has since become our national pride and set the tone for national development planning.

What would it have been without the biggest fire in the thorny issue of cheap autonomous housing that the 'kampongs' represented?

The Bukit Ho Swee fire may be truly marked as an *opportunity in a crisis, in a disaster*.

12

Pirate taxis

It was rather late at night and Pa, Mie, my two older sisters, I and my younger brother were in a pirate taxi that Pa had earlier waved down. Pa told the driver where we were going, which was Prince Charles Crescent where we lived. The driver knew the place. When we arrived, Pa gave the driver a sum of money, and the driver did not agree, both Pa and the driver started to raise their voices. Mie herded us out of the pirate taxi and Pa passed me on to Mie. He asked Mie to take us home while he sorted out the hassle. It appeared to me the situation would turn nasty.

Pirate taxis do not have or do not run on fare meters as our licensed taxis do these days. These were unlicensed freelancers, who picked up passengers at their own whim. Passengers had to flag them and agree on the proposed rate for the requested destination before they board. The rates for standard common routes were generally known and negotiable. Many of these drivers were hooligans who sometimes intimidate passengers for higher fares. They disappeared from the transportation system early in the seventies when NTUC

Comfort taxis came into being with strict regulations instituted to control the operation of taxis. Pirate taxis died a natural death.

When Pa got home, Mie asked him what happened and Pa simply brushed it off saying that he would not pay a cent more than the rate he would normally pay for that distance.

Singapore was early in its nation building during the time of the pirate taxis. Civil organisation could not happen overnight and until that happened, administration of law and order was difficult. Today we have licensed taxis operated by government-approved organisations where drivers undergo customer service training and meet licensing requirements. They publish flag-down charges and fares, and are fitted with automated meters so there is uniformity in the taxi system in Singapore. Expectations are no longer arbitrary as it was with pirate taxis. Alas, there is the predictability we are all so used to these days.

When Pa made the statement about not willing to pay more, I suspected there were threats and hard words exchanged between them. Knowing Pa, he would never entertain threats and knew enough about how to handle the rough tactics employed by these unlicensed pirate taxis.

Can we not fight fire (pirate taxis) with fire (forceful fare)? When two stones meet, they clash. How they, Pa and the pirate taxi operator, sorted out the issue, I will never know and can only surmise. In a broader sense, can pirate taxis, which thrive in lawlessness and chaos win, over a regime of modernisation, which demands law and order?

Times change, systems forcibly change out of necessity. Change is a big subject. Change is common and frequent in Singapore; we are a small young nation just like a young child in his age of innocence. We can almost parallel the timeline between them. As a man grows older, change slows. Alas! The nation outlives the man. The flesh is irreplaceable, the flesh corrupts, decays, fails; the nation replaceable by younger men who ultimately fails. We live in a temporal world, which for us is not a continuing city. There is an eternal world to come. Who will be there? Will you be there? Do you care?

13

Thai temple . . . and Religion

P a brought me to a Thai Buddhist temple at Silat Road. We walked up a steep slope to the temple reception area. It was a single storey concrete building with the front portion having a zinc-roofed extension. We went in, left our shoes before the foot-high threshold. Pa clasped his hands in reverence while addressing a Thai monk seated on a raised platform on one side of the rather large hall. He spoke in Thai as Pa approached him. Pa asked me to clasp my hands in similar fashion and introduced me. What they talked about was incomprehensible to me.

After some time, Pa bade farewell to the monk with the hand clasped and beckoned me to do the same. I understood this all to be greetings.

We put on our shoes and climbed up another slope to a rather magnificent temple building with a pointed rooftop, and entering the gate I could see a very large golden statue of a Buddha sitting cross-legged. We took out our shoes at the door of the worship hall. As Pa crossed the threshold, he knelt, clasped his hands in reverence, and bowed his head in worship. I followed suit not exactly knowing what to do.

The Thai Buddhist temple was Wat (meaning temple in Thai) Anandametyarama (was actually a word from an ancient Indian language known as Pali). 'Ananda' was a name while the middle syllable 'metya' came from the Pali 'metta' meaning loving kindness. 'Aram' simply meant shrine.

The chief abbot and several senior monks were from Thailand and spoke mostly Thai. They had picked up a few relevant words of Fujian to enable them to greet devotees and give a blessing. They often welcome Pa, as he was Thai Chinese and spoke in Thai. Pa was one local with whom they could have long chats and discussions.

That first visit was Pa's way of initiating me to his beliefs. From then, we walked some three miles from home to the temple every Sunday morning to attend Buddhist lessons termed Dharma class, and to worship at the general service. Singaporeans taught the Dharma class in English. There was a basic text in English and a definite syllabus. They told us that depending on our age category, the temple would invigilate the annual examinations. These were set in Colombo in Ceylon (now Sri Lanka) and they would send our completed papers to Colombo for assessment. Successful completion would enable us to move up the grade. Over the years, I collected several certificates and they were nice looking just like certificates we see these days: there was a red seal of the examining body, my name written with quill or similar instrument. They were nice and proud certificates to own, I have never had anything like these before.

Every Sunday we undertook to perform the five precepts, which were much like the ten commandments of the Old Testament in Christianity. The five were called *Pancasila* where 'panca' meant five: not to kill, not to steal, not to be intoxicated, not to lie, not to commit adultery. On special occasions, we would take on the ten precepts. I became careful not to kill anything that had life in it and I wondered whether we should treat plants as having life, since they grew. I began to watch for ants or creatures whenever I walked, just in case I stepped on them accidentally and terminate their lives. I just would not kill an ant, if it bothered me, I gently picked it up and threw it out the window, careful not to hurt or maim it.

When young, our lives were in our parents' hands: they shaped us, and they directed us in our goings and comings. In this case, I felt directed to a religion of my father but never had any qualms as I enjoyed all that I had undergone. The exposure I received allowed me to read beyond my age. I particularly enjoyed the Jataka stories from which we drew lessons for the Buddhist doctrine we studied. These stories provided a great deal of *wisdom* that had some influence in my *living*. They were like Proverbs in the Bible except they were very brief stories.

Walking three miles to the temple and the same distance home had nothing to do with our faith and zeal. We thoroughly enjoyed the trip, it was never just walking, there was skipping, short bursts of sprinting, looking into shop windows, studying signs, noticing the nurses living quarters, watching the Malayan Railway trains as we passed the tracks for a short distance of the way: our lively and curious minds fully occupied without end.

Performing the five precepts every week helped us work to keep a goodly life that only we knew whether it was 'walked'. It was all about *doing right and abstaining from wrong.* All seemed achievable but I struggled somewhat with lying not so much in telling a fib but more of not speaking up about a wrong.

My Buddhist studies in later years helped me understand that Buddhism was not a religion, as it has no God, therefore is not God-centric, very much like a belief in living unto oneself, without a starting point and having a dubious end-point: *nirvana*. We learned that it was a way of life. Again, in later years, as I questioned the philosophy behind Buddhism, I became rather disillusioned and that became a source of restlessness for many years. *The peace-seeking philosophy pleases and refreshes for a time like showers in a hot season that never quite reach the roots of life. There was just a lifeless, powerless belief shrouded in seeming peace and good works. It buys us entry, according to its cause and effect theory of* karma, *to an unknown future 'state' called* nirvana. *By all my calculations and reason, it is highly implausible.*

Endnotes

Religion is not merely about doctrine and precepts. It is not about an exuberant enthusiasm in outlook or good works, nor about intellectual speculation of what is or is not. It is the bridge between us here on earth, and the infinite, eternal beyond. Religion binds us, the sinful and corruptible man, with an immutable and righteous God.

In God's perfect creation, man in disobedience fell into sin, perversion, and transgression. Sin caused separation from a Holy God to which no reconciliation was possible unless a sacrifice offered in propitiation meets the demands of His righteous nature. God in all His mercy, characteristic of Himself provided His Son, the perfect Lamb of God, as the sacrifice that is sufficient to satisfy for the sins of the whole world, "*For God so loved the world, that he gave his only begotten Son, that whosoever believes in him should not perish, but have everlasting life.*" With God, there is a definite beginning, a clear purpose for being, and a certain comprehensible end. Salvation is a complete and perfectly packaged gift. This very act of the love of God binds us the failed man to Himself who is righteous, merciful, and unchanging.

14

My first school

The school Pa registered for me to enter was about a kilometre from home and we walked there. Pa took me along just to orientate me. My eldest sister Bao Yu, two years my senior was already studying there. The school was Jervois East School, taking its name from the street name along which it was located. Across its main entrance was another school, Jervois West School. Pa said it had Malay students. On the back of the school block across a wide patch of grass were four rows of 3-storied SIT flats and we lived in the furthermost block from school.

Registration was easy as Bao Yu was already in the school and that gave me preferential entry. Pa received a book list to purchase the school uniform, textbooks, and stationery at an appointed date. The school had boys and girls mixed in every class. It was a half-day school, so it had two sessions.

I understand Jervois is a French name. Many of our roads were named after famous persons who had a hand or contribution to Singapore. Jervois East School was an English co-ed school where

48

boys and girls mixed. This was quite normal. I had grown up among my sisters and believed I could handle them. Somehow up until now, I could not remember a single female classmate, be it the looks or name, all the way to primary three, about 9 years of age. Generally, my memory was that there were more boys. The students were all Chinese because the Malays went to Jervois West School, some two hundred meters from Jervois East.

Since it was a half-day school, it had two sessions each day, the morning, and afternoon. Students attend only one session. Each session had two classes of each level, that is, the primary-one level through to the primary-six level. Therefore, in each session, there were twelve classes; the school provided education for twenty-four classes, each averaging forty students. On a straight calculation, the school had nine hundred and sixty students.

Where we lived, and where my older sister went to school, determined the school I would enter. In short, it depended on circumstances of convenience: the older caring for the younger, using textbooks passed down from the older, walking distance to and from home, and ease of registration. Still, that did not matter. It was a time when education was not a matter of life and death. However, we were in nation building, there was hope in the future nation and our parents to have the *education that prepared us for the hopeful brighter future* in a socially unkind environment.

Endnotes
Our first and only school in life is God's Word.
In the beginning was the Word, and
The Word was with God, and
The Word was God . . . and
The Word was made flesh and dwelt among us,
Full of grace and of truth.

Our first lesson: "In the beginning
God created the heaven and the earth."
The world He created, was not self-existent,
It is God, the true God, who caused it to be.

Our continuing lesson: "For God so loved the world,
That he gave His only begotten Son,
That whosoever believeth in him
Should not perish,
But have everlasting life."
It is about Christ and about Him crucified for our sin.

Our enduring lesson: "Abide in me (Jesus) and I in you.
As the branch cannot bear fruit of itself,
Except it abide in the vine;
No more can you, except you abide in me."
The Father shall give you another Comforter,
That he may abide with you forever.

Our closing lesson, "Surely I come quickly."
The bodies of the unjust,
Shall by the power of Christ, be raised to dishonour;
The bodies of the just,
Shall by his Spirit, unto honour, and
Be made conformable to his own glorious body.

There shall be a day of judgment,
Both to deter all men from sin, and
For the greater consolation of the godly
In their adversity;
He will have that day unknown to men,
That they may shake off all carnal security.

Be watchful! Be vigilant!
You know not what hour the Lord will come.
Be ever prepared to say,
"Come, Lord Jesus, come quickly."

15

Starting school

P a brought me to school with the sling canvas bag containing the books and stationery. I wore new white socks, white shoes with laces, and my new uniform of dark blue shorts and saffron-coloured short-sleeved shirt. Following instructions to queue up, the headmaster read our names from a large book-like register. I heard my name called, and went to the queue assigned. A woman teacher escorted my group to the classroom. My class was 1A. I waved good-bye to Pa.

During recess, the teacher led us to the 'tuck shop'. Mie was waiting for me to help with money handling and purchase of food. The food stalls were lined along the inside perimeter of the tuck shop. One stall sold yellow cooked noodle; another sold candies, crackers, nuts and the like. Yet another sold red bean and green bean soup. The drinks stall sold glass bottled drinks and homemade coloured syrup drinks. Mie gave me ten cents and said that was to be my pocket money every day. She asked me to look about and decide what I would like to buy for food. I decided on green bean soup, it was something familiar as we had it at home on weekends. Mie said it was 'cooling' and therefore good for the body. My bowl of green beans soup was five cents, and I collected a change with the ten cents I gave the vendor. I sat down on a bench that was parallel to the long table, and ate the beans and drank the soup. I bought a large prawn cracker with the remaining five cents. All this while Mie was keeping an eye on me and said not a word about my choice of food. I took that to mean she approved of it.

Later in the year as I became familiar with the school environs, became more settled into the system, assumed more ease at trying things out, one thing that became a problem was my white school shoes. They became dirty within an hour of getting to school. The teacher usually called us to the front whenever she needed to use large teaching aids. We sat on the floor, cross-legged with the outside of our white canvas shoes resting on the floor. When we stood up to return to our desks and seats, my shoes darkened by the dirt and dust from the floor left me wondering what to do. I had only a pair and washed them on weekends when there was no schooling. White chalk from the green chalkboard ledge became the solution: I rolled a short white chalk over the darkened outside of my shoes to cover the dirt marks.

Pa had always impressed upon us the importance of education. He always reminded that he did not have one, and that had affected his place and portion in life. He was not ashamed to compare himself to his brothers who had the education and rose to better positions in life, economically speaking. While he was able to provide for our schooling, he expected us to do well at it so that we in turn would be able to ride up the economic ladder when we go out into society to work.

Starting school was a thrilling experience that initiated me into the unknown world of knowledge acquisition, skills development, and social interaction in an environment where I met and studied with others of the same age. It was the beginning of a memorable life outside of home, filled with joy, discovery, inquiring, and learning essential to my formative years. *It was double joy, one at home, and another in school.*

Endnotes

Schooling has a system, teaching has its pedagogy, and learning or acquiring skills has a process. They work together to provide a sound effective organisation to produce educated students. In our case, the primary education prepares students for secondary education in order to receive further education and training at tertiary levels, ultimately to generate a workforce that meets the economic demands for different disciplines/trades. As with all organisations there are rules to adhere to, failing which the consequences trigger.

The school uniforms we wore, the socks, and shoes, the haircut, the homework, tests, discipline, and conduct, were all necessary for the functioning of the school as an organisation. Tardy students received punishment, those caught gambling, or smoking received humiliation before the whole school through caning. Further severe offences warranted expulsion.

Deterrence played a silent and influential hand in our early school life and social life. Call it a hedge if you like. The consequence of breaching the hedge was punishment: caning, expulsion, standing in the corner, fines, and penalties for offences of all sorts.

Many live in obedience to the law more from fear of punishment, from necessity than from love, and a sense of righteousness. Hence, there is no peace except in humble obedience to authority because it is right to do so.

Perhaps, school was a 'safe' experimental ground to work on policies that affect society as a whole, for the young progresses to become adults ultimately. The young also become a piece of our economy, our political thinking, our workforce, the families of the future; the experiments become a learning base to craft future policies that perpetuate the society we would create, that is sustainable and enduring. We build a society not in a year or some years, it takes decades. Who can see what lies ahead? The system cannot be force-fed: we cannot clone from another nation, another economic, social environment, as the dynamics are different. We can learn from others. A paradigm shift has again taken place when we now encourage teachers to *teach less* and let children *learn more.*

16

Free Milk . . . for the Malnourished

After the first few months in school, there was a student health check in the school hall. We queued up to have our weight taken, our heights measured, and our hearts and lungs heard. We returned to class and the form mistress called out some names, my name was among those called and she informed us to go down to the office everyday just before the recess time, to drink 'free' milk because we were not so 'strong'. This would begin from the next day.

The next day ten minutes before recess, we went down to queue for our milk. The school attendant took a big scoop and poured the hot creamy white milk into each of our cups as we held them. We finished all of it, and no waste allowed. It had an awful smell about it and was tasteless. I faithfully went through this ritual for the rest of the year.

After this routine went on for a month or so, we became familiar with the procedures, and helped the school attendant to fill the pail with tap water for washing the used cups. We also helped hand out the cups, etc., to the children. One day, I worked up enough courage to ask the school attendant what the teacher meant when she said we were not 'strong'. He said 'not enough vitamins'. I did not understand 'vitamins' and pursued to question him. Finally, he explained that I did not have enough of the right food in my body; the milk was to help provide the inadequate food.

Since the health check was rather basic, I surmised the weight was the telling sign for being categorised as malnourished. Over the rest of that year, the milk had done its work and I did not have to go through the routine the following year. In fact, I did not remember any of us having to drink milk the following year.

Was milk drinking policy meant for those in the first year of schooling, as we were rather delicate in frame, and to allow us to get to a level footing with healthier children? I never pursued the matter and never found out, if ever there was a reason for it.

Endnotes

Young children, growing and full of energy must feed well and get to a level footing with healthier children. Healthy minds need healthy bodies.

17

School pocket money

F or much of our primary school life our pocket money was ten cents a day, enough for a tiny bowl of noodles with some slices of fish cake. For drinks, we used the water fountain or the tap at the sink in the tuck shop (canteen). Alternatively, we were able to get a bowl of green or red bean soup, and a large piece of *keropok* (prawn crackers).

Sometimes we saved half of the pocket money for the following day and enjoyed slightly wider helpings or choices of food.

As we walked to school every day, the meagre pocket money bought enough food until we went home for lunch or dinner.

Just to give you an idea of the value of money then, a fried kway teow (flat noodles) with egg, and cockles from a regular hawker stall outside the school tuck shop cost thirty cents. At school, the portions shrank significantly in size and the prices were different by a wide berth. Children generally eat less relative to adults.

A glass bottle of RC Cola and other unbranded coloured fizzy drinks cost ten cents. The Coca Cola might have cost fifteen cents. We could never afford a Coca Cola in school.

We received just adequate pocket money according to our situational affordability, a case of *limited resources*.

We received enough pocket money to allow us to make *need*ful *choices*, though *limited*, a case of *efficient* resource *allocation*.

We had enough to *optimize* on food, by *choice* of the free water resource from the tap or fountain.

It was all early lessons in economics. It was unintended but *scarcity* forced its hand on us all.

Endnotes

Economics is the science that deals with production, the distribution, and consumption of goods and services, or the material welfare of humankind. That definition fits in well with what we learned in life.

18

Arithmetic . . . one of the 3Rs

We were told by the arithmetic teacher to collect lots of ice cream sticks and metal bottle caps from the tuck shop. We were to bring them to class the next day. During recess, I ran out to the tuck shop with my friend and headed for the drinks stall to pick up bottle caps strewn about the stall. Once done, we put them all in a plastic bag. We next headed for the garbage bin to pick up the used ice cream sticks, still sticky with melting ice cream. We washed the sticks clean and got them into another plastic bag.

The next day during the arithmetic lesson, the teacher asked us all to bring the bottle caps we had collected and put them in a shoebox. She instructed us to do the same for the ice cream sticks to go into another shoebox. She next took out a self-standing giant bead counter and stood it in the front to teach us how to add. We each then collected ten bottle caps from the shoebox and returned to our seats.

She next wrote out a problem for us to solve collectively. It was simply:

$2 + 3 = $ _. We each took out two bottle caps and another three and totalled them. She asked for the answer and we gave it in unison as '5'. That was how adding started and in subsequent lessons we learnt subtraction, all in primary one, at age six and seven. We did the same with ice cream sticks. There was homework for that lesson. It was set out on the board for us to copy into our exercise books.

Simple teaching methods made things clear for me. It was the excitement of activity, and the simple 'teach-see-do' process, that made arithmetic easy and fun. I went on to top my school in Mathematics, the later name for Arithmetic, when I was in primary six, the final year at Jervois East.

The general tenet of education was the three R's. Arithmetic was fundamental not in just learning to count—add, subtract, multiply, and divide—but to apply them to solve problems in a buying/selling situation, problems that required an indirect deductive way of finding the solution, and solving mathematical puzzles. They were all fun to one as me, who loved exploring, and solving problems. Arithmetic was totally enriching.

There is a Chinese saying: "When I hear, I forget; when I see, I understand; when I do, I remember." *Arithmetic is a 'do' subject.*

19

Tests

The teacher explained that she was passing out the test papers for a particular subject. There were some blanks to fill in with the 'helping' words provided at the top of the questions. It was all without fuss, we simply followed instructions, and when we had completed the paper, we were to wait for the others to complete theirs. At the end of the allotted time, the teacher asked everyone to stop writing and went about collecting the papers. She then allowed us to leave the classroom.

This was my first experience at a test. I did not remember any tension or stress. It was like another piece of work that we often do in class except this one was rather solemn, no one spoke or laughed, or coughed, and it was all so quiet—indeed very unusual.

This test was for the second term of my primary one session. There was no test for the first term. I suppose we had not learnt enough in the first term. Over time, I learnt that tests were a routine that occurred two or three times before the end of each term. They were important and the results recorded in the report book, which

Pa ultimately would see and examine. I was answerable for the outcomes of the tests and the form master's comments.

An aside: in later years, Mie let us each eat a half-boiled egg before we leave for school to take the major tests we call examinations. Mie said the eggs would make our minds more alert and were anyway, also nutritious. For us, eggs were a luxury and to take them before examinations was a real treat. We loved half-boiled eggs with dark soy sauce and pepper powder.

———◆◇◆———

Tests and examinations are necessary to evaluate a child's abilities, aptitudes, and skills concerning the knowledge taught. Sometimes the pedagogy emphasises rote learning and memory work, while at other times, understanding and application. As young children, we have little understanding about the science of education and learning. We did what we were told and taught, and prepared for examinations by revising those lessons. Examinations assessed our learning accordingly. Passing or doing well in examinations did not necessarily mean that we were brilliant. It was an indication that we learned well what the education system taught. *Did the system teach us effectively?* I like to believe so.

Tests served to bring pressure to bear upon our efforts at our studies. Some tension is often a good thing in that it 'tests' understanding, stretches the learning, and activates the skills that enlarges our abilities in taking in knowledge. *Just as gold goes through the furnace to refine, tests serve as that furnace to refine our attitudes and skills, in order to learn well.*

Endnotes

In life, we can trust God to test and strengthen our faith, and to hone our character to be like Him, prepared for good works, and fit for His pleasure.

Behold, I have refined thee, but not with silver; I have chosen thee in the furnace of affliction.

20

First Report Book

Towards the end of the second term in primary 1, I collected my report book from the teacher as my name was called out. The teacher wanted me to bring it home to let Pa see it and to sign his name in the column provided. My position in class was 24 out of 40 students. There was one red mark, all else were in blue. I had nine marks out of twenty for comprehension.

At the end of the third and final term, the teacher updated the same book and issued it again. My position had moved to fifth and I had no red marks. The teacher had written out some remarks on the report card. I could not understand at that time, as the word was long: 'over-confident'. Neither did Pa. he had to consult his English-Thai dictionary.

For Pa, a red mark was bad and required his immediate attention. The number of marks I received relative to the maximum attainable marks gave indication of how poorly I had performed. I learnt not to collect a red mark again to avoid having to answer for it. Low marks were also not acceptable.

The first report book was an important one. It sets all the ground rules for how all future reports should look like: no red marks, no low scores, position in class within the top ten—though that bar moved up with the years—and the form master's report on my performance and character must show no evidence of weakness or slackening.

Was that a tall order? The thought never entered my mind. I simply enjoyed all that I did and had to do. Life just happily and energetically chugged along; I never had to fail those ground rules that set the *standard* for me as far as schooling was concerned. Reports at periodic intervals helped me to know *what* was the *expectation* and my job was to take care of the *how* to meet it.

21

Pa checks school work

When Pa returned from work, he took his shower, ate his dinner, and asked me to bring my schoolbag over to him. We sat on the floor, pulled out the contents from the schoolbag on to a low worktable. He looked at each of the exercise books, as that was where school work was done; that was also where I had homework to be handed in the next day for the form master to mark, meaning to check and validate my answers to confirm my understanding. Pa would question me on any unusual markings such as an 'X', which indicated a mistake, for which I had to make a correction at the bottom of the page. He next wanted to know what was incorrect in the first place.

You will remember that Pa did not receive schooling, and yet he checked my schoolbag every day and went over the work I did at school, as well as the homework that I must hand in the next day. He really had no idea what was going on, but had such interest that he learned what I learnt in school. He was having a *belated schooling*. I was as serious in sharing, as he was interested in knowing. This routine was daily as long as Pa had no need to go out in the evening.

Sharing my schoolwork with Pa reinforces my understanding and memory of what the teacher taught at school. It was a form of repetition that was fundamental to recall which was drawn upon, and made available to the brain for use in future associated application.

It was a joy to share knowledge with Pa: he was so interested and hungered for it. The true value for me was Pa loved me enough to be interested, and since he missed schooling, the best means available to him was to have me tell him what I have done at school through the schoolwork. *Love always finds the best available means.*

Endnotes

Be thou diligent to know the state of thy flocks, and look well to thy herds.

In fact, the old English word for diligent is *diligo* meaning to love. Fathers as shepherds must *love* to know the state of his flocks.

22

Pa's devotion to religion

Pa woke up at five every morning when all else is still and quiet except for the early birds chatting in the trees. It was all still dark and shadowy. He would do his toileting and have a cold shower as we did not have or could we afford water heaters then. All that would take half an hour and then he would change into neat clothes, usually a well-ironed short-sleeved shirt and long pants.

He would then go up to his altar where a cross-legged Buddha statue and several other images were organized. He would burn three joss ticks, held them in a clasping position, moved his lips in silent worship, and stuck them into the pile of slightly hardened ash in the little brass cauldron. Clasping his hands in worship, he would silently speak his prayer. Once done, he would from a small round tray, pick up an amulet that had a long thick string that held it. He prayed over it and hung it around his neck, tucked it behind his shirt front buttons so the amulet rested on his chest hidden from view.

He next pulled out a two-dollar note and then went into the room to leave it on the dresser top for mum to use for marketing. That marketing allowance increased when times were better. Pa then checked himself, went to the main door, pulled back the latch, turned the door knob to open the door, and when he was outside the house, he pulled shut the self-locking door. I could hear a short push and pull to check the fastness of the lock. I would move over to the bedroom window to see Pa's back as he turned the block to cross the road.

I watched Pa daily in his routine morning activity always quietly behind a slightly gaping door of our bedroom. I have been a light sleeper and an early riser all my life. Curiosity and a lively mind may have a lot to do with it.

It was not normal to shower in warm water as that required boiling a kettleful and mixing it with cold tap water. Boiling water meant the attendant fuel cost, and it took time as well.

I had asked Pa on one occasion about the object of his prayer, and for what he was praying. Pa said he prayed to Buddha, thankful for his portion in life, asked for provision and protection for his family and himself.

The quietude of the early morning hours when all din depart, where feelings and zeal are without edge, when one in humility communes with one's own heart, with one who is our Maker, are the sweetest. We must go apart and be with our Lord each day, be in His blessed presence, be at the Master's feet to listen to the sacred thoughts that spring forth from Him and shed in our hearts, simply wait in humble faith lapping up the assurance of His love. The insurmountable yesterday overcame—one now braces with renewed strength and hope drawn from the Maker's love—for another day. Strength is conceived in quietness, in solitude, free from the rush and toil, from the hustle and bustle.

Pa in his religious devotion had been reverentially thankful for life and asked for survival and security needs—no supplication for more, fully contented with all he had and will receive. *Gratefulness drove contentment.*

Endnotes

Pa devotedly served other ineffectual gods. He found that out in due time and in his later years placed his trust and devotion to the one and only true God. God saw his devotion to false gods, had compassion and mercy for him, and redirected that devotion to Himself.

God that made the world and all things therein,
Seeing that he is Lord of heaven and earth,
Dwells not in temples made with hands;
Not worshipped with men's hands, as though he needs anything,
Seeing he gives to all life, and breath, and all things;
Has made of one blood all nations of men for to dwell on all the face of
*   the earth,*
Has determined before the times before appointed, and the bounds of their
*   habitation;*
That they should seek the Lord, if haply they might feel after him,
Find him, though he is not far from every one of us:
For in him we live, and move, and have our being; as certain also of your
*   own poets have said, for we are also his offspring.*

23

Mie's carrot and the stick

When we were all of school going age, my brother and I would go out of home to play. Mie gave us a few simple rules to adhere:

- Shower after we return home from school.
- Take our lunch.
- Complete the day's school homework.
- Revise the textbook from the beginning until the latest lesson.
- Read up for the next day's lessons.
- Go out to play but must stay within earshot. Should she call, we were to respond immediately otherwise she would not allow us to go out and play the next time.

By then, we had Bao Yu, Zhu, I, my brother Tian Cai, sister Lian, and a toddler sister Zuan, in that order. Mie had grouped the boys and the girls. If we were out running about the wide, open spaces near the house, there were only Tian Cai and I. The girls tended to play their own games at home or at the stairways. It was a silent understanding that girls do not go out to play unless accompanied by Mie and/or Pa.

Mie was a natural manager. She understood that privilege begets responsibility, which begets accountability. There were unpleasant consequences when accountability fails to meet responsibility. That was the simple mandate any young child can understand; nothing more nothing less. There was no list of 'do' and 'do not' to reckon with.

When *responsibility and accountability* met their conditions, I learnt also that *reward and recognition* kicked in. I thrived on them all the way from age three until twelve. They virtuously reinforce each other.

Endnotes
Whenever we begin a task,
We must bring it to end.
Whatever we begin to do,
We must commit to complete.
That is perfecting.

24

School fees

I t was that time at the beginning of each month to pay school fees. Teacher had a large register that contained the names of students in her class. She used it to mark the daily attendance as well as the monthly school fees payment. When she called my name, I went up to her. As I stood next to her, I spoke softly to explain that Pa had requested a deferment until the middle of the month. She understood and asked me to return to my seat.

From the time I was in Primary two, paying my school fees had been consistently late by a half-month and sometimes a month. By Primary two, Pa had to pay school fees for eldest sister Bao Yu, who was in Primary 4, for me and for younger brother who was in Primary one. Second sister Zhu, did not qualify for schooling due to her deficiency. It was up to each of us to explain to the teacher of our situation. Whenever Pa had the means of paying the fees on time, we were very glad to redeem our past deferments.

I learned some things from Pa through these apparently embarrassing moments. One was *honestly* to explain the reason for being unable to fulfil our obligation, in this case, prompt payment of fees. The second was to *propose a plan* of payment within our means, ultimately to fulfil that obligation. Finally, we must *keep promises*, by paying our overdue fees.

From an even bigger perspective, our God also the Divine Creditor has released our indebtedness to Him because Christ had paid for all our sins on the cross. He redeemed us by His blood, efficacious and acceptable of God as propitiation for our indebtedness.

Endnotes

When you vow a vow unto God, defer not to pay it; for He *has* no pleasure in fools: pay that which you have vowed. Better *is it* that you should not vow, than that you should vow and not pay.

Owe no man any thing, but to love one another: for he that loveth another hath fulfilled the law.

Forgive us our debts, as we forgive our debtors.

25

Speedy Gonzales

Mie was busy with house chores and needed me to run an errand for her: thirty cents of raw three-layered pork. She gave me the money and instructed me from which store to buy. I was excited, started my imaginary motorcycle by making the vroom sound as though revving and ready to scoot in quick time. Additionally, I exclaimed "Hiba, hiba. Speedy Gonzales to the rescue" and off I went. Mie shouted after me to be careful.

I bought the pork wrapped with used newspaper, paid the money and ran off towards home. As I sped across the road, something hit and I did not remember a thing. When I gained consciousness, a tall well-dressed man carried me in his arms. He asked exactly where I lived as though he knew the address but was not very familiar with the area. I looked about to gather my orientation and pointed to the direction where our house was. As we neared, he let me down and asked me to lead him there. We got to our house on the second floor of block 65. Mie saw us approach and wondered what had happened. The tall man explained the episode to Mie, and she appeared to be satisfied and the man departed.

When B & W television first came on, and we were able to peep into other peoples' houses to watch some programs, Speedy Gonzales had always caught my fancy. He was a little mouse in a Mexican sombrero. He runs like the wind, his legs would run up a whirl and he was off. He would come to an immediate stop when necessary. He was always dashing about to perform heroics like helping people in distress or getting things from one place to another in the nick of time to salvage a situation, save a life or prevent a disaster.

I always loved errands and always hoped for more, simply because I loved running. It was a joy to use my limbs and my speed . . . I was like Speedy Gonzales.

In the event above, I had an accident with the tall man's car. Apparently, he had also stopped in time so that the impact was not disastrous. The car knocked me unconscious and there were no cuts, no bleeding, just skin surface scratches. He checked with the street vendors, several of whom knew who I was, where I lived and provided him with the block number 65. The man explained to Mie the incident and Mie acknowledged that I was also at fault due to my love for running. The matter ended agreeably and the man took his leave.

I got a mild scolding from Mie as she checked to make sure I was all in one piece. She reminded me to stop at road crossings and not to dash across without looking out first. Although at that time I appeared physically in order, it was years later that my left rib cage had a gentle inward dent. It is still there more visibly obvious. No bones were broken and the rib cage had protected my essential organs! What Providence!

The event above did not end the forays of Speedy Gonzales. Another time was worse, I was carrying a pot of hot coffee, and half way home, it started to rain heavily. I ran as fast as I possibly could for I did not have an umbrella then. While crossing the road, I ran into a cyclist, who like me was speeding to dry shelter. He did not stop and went off. I had about half the coffee left in the pot, some mild bleeding scratches, and profuse bleeding just outside and below the lower lip. The lower lip scar remained until this day. No harm done but I received the usual scolding.

I thought the car driver was responsible enough to send me home and did the necessary to return me to my house. It was not a hit-and-run situation. He made sure I was all right and took time to restore me to my family. In front of Mie, there was no pointing of fingers at me for causing it.

Mie was also very cordial and open, expressing I was also at fault for being reckless. She was thankful that he brought me home safely. She made no demands on the man.

There was a sense that everyone meant well for everyone else, a sense of simple human trust. Any issue could sort out amicably, and there would be fair play. Fair is about the absence of prejudice or dishonesty, not judging for the benefit of self-gain but free from such bias. Fairness from the driver begets fairness from Mie.

As for the cyclist, he possibly cared more for himself or did not think I was hurt badly enough to need assistance. Whichever way, I was alive and grateful.

Responsible people do not run away from a problem or blame it on someone else. They own up to it gracefully and obligingly. The goodwill generated was notable and high-minded.

26

The Gorgeous Flood

O ne morning as I walked to school, it started to rain and I was caught in it a little. Throughout the whole morning, the rain poured heavily with no sign of abating. Thunders, and lightning and ceaseless pounding of the rain made the morning look gloomy. No running out in the field, we stayed indoors. By mid morning, during the session recess, the tuck shop was beginning to flood to the ankle. Looking out to the car park, it was literally under water. It was all rather chaotic and the headmaster used his loud hailer to instruct the students to move quickly back to our classes on the second floor. When class ended at about twelve thirty, the ground floor had been flooded up to about my knee as I waited for Pa to fetch me.

This flood was a fun and novel event for me, I had never seen anything like it, and very soon, when Pa arrived to fetch me, I got to walk in the floodwaters. The rain had trickled to a light drizzle when Pa arrived at the tuck shop. He took my schoolbag, tied the strap about his neck, and held my right hand. As we walked gingerly in the flood, I suddenly slipped into a shallow drain hidden from view. Pa immediately pulled me up by my hand, which he held. I laughed away and Pa decided it was time to pull me up on his back as he ploughed through the floodwaters. Once we got home, Pa left me with Mie and went back to school to fetch Bao Yu whose senior class ended half an hour after mine.

The downpour was truly the longest we had ever experienced. All was well in our neighbourhood except for the death of a young child washed away in a large monsoon drain. That was news the next day. The school, erected at a spot lower than the residential area, naturally succumbed to flooding. By the next day when we returned to school, the flood had subsided and we could see that the school field was not usable with large uneven patches of grass and puddles. Waterlogged it was.

Whenever it rained, we stayed in the rain for as long as we could get away with it before Mie ordered us off it. We simply enjoyed the rain striking against our heads and faces, and getting all drenched, I suppose. Why not play in it since we were already soaked. It was not that we had rain every day.

However, the rain was always fun for us whether staying indoors or out. I could kneel on the wooden sofa in the living hall of our house for hours just looking out at the rain. It had a certain attraction for me just watching it come down in such a regular pattern, and out of the clouds though I cannot see how that happened. I often imagined there were water tanks that contained holes on their bottom, and hidden in the clouds. Then there was the question about how the clouds held up the water, and when on a regular bright day, I could see that clouds moved, and have heard that the winds blow to move them. Who blew the clouds? Who gave orders for the tanks to fill up, and for the holes to open so that the rain came on? Where did the water come from in the first place? Years later when we learnt about geography and science, they dashed my theory to smithereens! Ignorance was what I had to show for all the curious imaginations.

Floods can be destructive especially when the rain incessantly poured at a rate faster than the waters could drain off. *Can we slow down the rain and quicken the drain?* Then, we will never ever have a flood!

The flood was a new phenomenon and was enjoyable. However, with the death of the child in the news, we felt sorry for it. There was definite danger, and every care employed to overcome it.

Endnotes

Has the rain a father? or who hath begotten the drops of dew?

He causes the vapours to ascend from the ends of the earth; he makes lightnings for the rain; he brings the wind out of his treasuries.

He binds up the waters in his thick clouds; and the cloud is not rent under them.

He binds the flood from overflowing; and the thing that is hid brings he forth to light.

The greatest flood in history thousands of years ago, recorded in the Bible wiped out civilisation. God caused it to come upon man because man was disobedient and sinful. Evil was so pervasive and unrelenting on earth that God took them away with a flood so great. Only and his family who were righteous lived on to start over again. God promised man that never would He send another flood as that. Still, they would sin and miss the mark, God's standard. That promise stays on and you can see God's love whenever you see the rainbow after a rain.

27

Now the Bomb

After the flood waters had subsided, the water-logged field firmed up with two days of strong sun: we were all raring to step on it again. As children let out of restraint, we ran the field playing 'police and thieves', catching, or marbles at the sand pit. Upon seeing an object in the sand pit, one of the students alerted the headmaster. He came to have a look and immediately told everyone to keep off the sand pit. Soon after, staff set up iron pickets about 25 yards from the pit all around and striped plastic tapes circled the pickets, marking out the off-limits cordon.

In a few hours, the police and military officers were at the scene to study the object in the sand pit. Finally, with a team of khaki-clad me in helmets, they removed it from the scene.

The following day, the school informed that the object in the sand pit was an unexploded mortar bomb. It warned us that if we were to spot such an object or any other unusual object, we must immediately report it to the school office. Apparently, the flood of a few days before had floated the mortar bomb to the school compound.

The bomb was probably like the firecracker that I knew. The latter was a little gunpowder wrapped about with many layers of red paper with a fuse from the heart of the gunpowder to the outside, certainly a quite harmless mini-bomb. The mortar bomb on the other hand was many times larger, and made of metal, which broke into little pieces of sharp metal upon explosion. The force of explosion sent the sharp metal pieces flying at high speed and penetrating shelters and human bodies. The bomb can kill. The bomb was used in war, and firecrackers used in Chinese New Year celebration.

That was an unexpected outcome of the flood. We all came to know a little bit about the mortar bomb, and when we should encounter one, what to do about it. One gorgeous flood brought on an exciting bomb. *Early life was much like that: parcels of surprising gifts one after another.* We can open them up and grin with a broad smile of 'surprise' to enjoy their contents or we can look 'dejected' that they cannot be enjoyed. Perhaps, the element of surprise and curiosity that a child sees is what makes all events appear gorgeous and thrilling. As we mature, we have probably lost touch with '*surprise*'. We are comfortable with predictability; we get what we look for.

28

Cows and Goats

There was a large open field beside our block of flats all the way to Jervois West School. Nearly once a month in the evening, Indian herders, dressed in simple tee shirts and girded loins would carry stiff reeds, much like canes to prod a flock of about thirty goats and a herd of about fifty cows. They brought these animals to the field to graze. Counting them from our veranda was a fun thing. Some cows were brown, some white, and others in white and black patches. The herders would shout in Tamil and the scene was one of chaos. Soon they drove the cows out of that field and went back to the Tiong Bahru/Red Hill area.

What the animals left behind was a lot of bad smell from the patties of dark green-looking cow dung and black pellet-like goat droppings that filled the field and parts around the blocks of flats where we live. Several middle-aged women, who immediately after the animals were gone, went about with large paper bags and scraper to scoop up the cow dung. They did not appear interested in the goats' droppings.

***

The women who collected the cow dung sold it as manure to vegetable farmers for use as fertiliser. They had value contrary to what we thought, just useless dung that smelled bad, and littered the nice green fields. They left the goat dung alone as they were probably too little and worthless.

This grazing scene was something we all enjoyed. I remember I could stand at the kitchen veranda watching the episode from start to finish, soaking in the pleasure of the activity, and doing nothing else. Few cows had horns. Most cows were medium-sized, quite young still. Around their hips, they all had a round marking painted on. This, I later found out identified ownership of the herd. They all had funny looking mouths that became funnier when they chewed the grass. Their legs were skinny and ugly. I imagined their hooves to be shoes. They were not well-fed, rather emaciated, not starved certainly. I even thought they must be Indian cows.

Just in an hour of watching, observing and imagining, there was so much to learn about the cows, the goats, the Indian herders, the dung collectors, the dung and its value, the ravaged fields and their recovery only to repeat in a month's time.

Things were very like that, they come, and they go away, to come again unless something changed. True enough some years later, the fields were gone and eighteen-storey flats took root. The cows and goats stopped coming, we missed the Indian voices of the herders. I would rather have them than the flats.

More than thirty years later, all the slab-block eighteen-storey flats were gone. In its place, modern expensive condominiums laid their foundations.

Endnotes

It looks like the cows and goats will not return.
The Indian herders and the dung collectors with them
Where have they gone?

To greener pastures to graze?
When greens are disappearing everywhere?
When brown earth closing in fast?

29

Community big screen

In those youthful days, we had a community centre not far from where we live. Behind the centre was an open-air badminton court. This is where the centre would screen black and white movies ran on reels and projected onto a large screen. The sound was always bad and unclear. People from all around the area gathered there to watch the movie screened. They bring plastic sheets, or paper bags or old newspapers to sit on. It was a fun evening out as Mie and the girls, Pa and the boys just got together around the screen. I had no idea what those movies were. Just being there was quite an event. There was the hullabaloo in setting up the big screen. The poor and funny sound system, and whenever the film reel went off-track, they drew laughs from the audience. Sometimes the organizers had trouble resuming the runs and we ended up with no movie to watch.

This big screen movie was a community service and did not cost anything. It was round about the time of black and white television. The whole event had little meaning for most of us but was something the neighbourhood did together. We had the opportunity to meet some of our neighbours and allowed the adults to keep in touch.

When people do not own a private screen at home, we get this huge community screen for a great number of people. It was like a community evening outing after dinner. People were more leisurely in their ways in that they enjoyed the simple means of coming together, a sense of being equal and sharing a common program as they gathered.

The big community screen did not spell out its intentions. It was but a means of bringing people of a locality, a neighbourhood together who shared some commonality, some similarity in race, social standing, culture, and heritage. It was a poor means—highly disorganised and misconceived—focused on bad entertainment, the grosser 'want' than on a *higher unifying purpose.*

30

Great World City

Great World City was an amusement park. There were eating stalls, cinemas, level tram rides, short ghost train rides, games, and the like. I liked the cotton candy as Pa bought one to share with us all. In the park were four cinemas: Atlantic Theatre, Canton Cinema, Sky Theatre, and the Globe Theatre. These were rather large cinemas, with the former two screening Chinese movies and the latter two mostly English movies. It was kind of a standard thing for us that Mie took the girls with her to watch the Chinese movies, and Pa took the boys with him to the English movies. Pa bought two tickets, one for himself and other was for Tian Cai and me to share a seat.

Later as we were growing up, I learnt that there were other 'Worlds' in Singapore. Great World was the nearest to our house and was the only entertainment centre known to us. The other entertainment worlds were Gay World, Happy World, and Beauty World.

———⟨≷⟩———

They were amusement parks. People bought tickets to enter them. When in there, people paid to ride a ghost train, ride the carousel, tried their hands at throwing balls into holes in the wall and winning some cheap furry toys, and so on. Visitors to these amusement parks were there for entertainment to get away from reality, perhaps, or to while away their time. The amusement parks provided seemingly meaningless activity that gratified for the evening, nothing lasting; the entertained then return to their homes to rest and prepare for another day.

Work . . . **Amusement** . . . **Rest**. That was for the adults.

School . . . *homework* . . . *play* . . . **Amusement** . . . *review for school next day* . . . **Rest**. Children had a little more to do, and it was not 'Work'.

31

New World of TV

Black and white television was in vogue and very few families were able to afford them. Usually at about six in the late afternoon, my brother and I would stand near a window of a neighbour's house on the ground floor to peek through their laced curtains to watch the program that was on the TV. Occasionally, some neighbours were annoyed and told us to go away or block our view with a cardboard. Ingenious as we were, we sometimes peeped through the letter-drop slit on the front door. On a few occasions, we had saliva spitted into our eyes from the other end of the slit.

We were amazed at the TV particularly with the cartoon programs like Bugs Bunny, to Elmer Fudd, the Road Runner, Speedy Gonzales, Mr. Magoo, and Tweety.

There was a certain amount of curiosity about how a box could produce all these movies but that was not at all important. It was what we were able to get out it, and there was always more.

In those early days of television, the antenna was a wide 'V' type placed atop the TV. A little later, antennae with horizontal 'sticks hung outside the house for better reception. The TV introduced to us the quality on the little screen that was many times better than the community big screen that swayed with the wind distorting the pictures on it. The film reels broke down often and was an annoyance, and the sound system was poorly audible. Besides, the pictures were old and meant more for adults. The TV was entertainment for us young ones, the cartoons were what we went for as they screened them between six and seven in the evening. It suited us as it was just before dinner. After the cartoons, we would rush home for shower, dinner, and then on to schoolwork.

Be the TV, at the community centre or at a cinema, it was a large screen with a single movie watched by a large number of people congregating in one public place. The TV changed all that. It was a little box with a glass screen watched by one or a few people in the comfort of home, a private place and who do not all have to watch the same program, they can watch whatever they pleased by simply turning a dial to a channel of choice. Ten homes could be watching ten different programs simultaneously. *This must be marked and remembered as truly a paradigm shift.*

32

Our First B&W

In my first term in primary 3, I came in the third position in class, and in a casual discussion, Pa asked whether I can be the first in class in the next term. I said I would try. As an enticement, he said he would get a television should I come in first in class in the second term. He knew I was fascinated with the black and white television available then.

I aimed to be first in class and made it. Pa kept his promise and bought one. He did not have the money and took out a hire purchase arrangement so that he could pay by instalments, which would make his outlay more manageable.

I had my first black and white television, and it belonged to everyone else at home and I would invite my friends over at six in the evening to learn Bahasa Kebangsaan or watch cartoons. We no longer had to peep into other people's houses to watch the cartoons.

Before the advent of TV, we had the radio at home that had some bulbs in it to power it. That came from the wire that tapped electricity from the two-pin power socket. The radio was where we listened to music, stories, and drama. Later on, we had the Rediffusion box that did not need a power socket but ran from a wire that led outside the house. Just sound varied to animate a scene, an action, that we imagined we heard.

With our own B & W TV, a new discipline was in place so that we retained our existing pattern of shower, dinner, schoolwork, and bedtime. There had to be scheduled time for learning Bahasa Kebangsaan, watching the news, enjoying cartoons. Mie allowed us to watch movies only on weekends. We found out that the TV station actually showed a list of the TV programs for the day. We found some interesting shows but were restricted until we completed our primary duties and activities.

When we had radio and Rediffusion, we listened and imagined. The sound we received had to be clear and understandable for us to translate the intended message to our young impressionable minds. We had to process the sound, the voice, the storyline. The radio storyteller did a great job through those elements to express the entire dynamics attendant on the scene in the story, and evoked the precise modicum and progression of tension, awe, or fear to create an almost life-like portrayal that mirrored the scenes in our minds. What great powers the storyteller had!

The TV provided a third dimension, sight. We not only heard and imagined, we now heard, saw, and imagined more precisely. However, the TV fed us the imagination; it did not come from us. *The TV gave us more of the sensibility: we imagined less, and anticipated more. The attention shifted from the processing of sound to that of processing sight.* We grew accustomed to it; that may have changed our attitudes to listening.

The art of *listening* had been lost and this is reflected in the way of *talking*—short, direct, quick—with the sole purpose of relaying a message. The patience associated with listening is not common as can be seen in the 'let us get to the point' or 'the point is' sense of edginess, of snappiness, of an abruptness almost as though agitated, which makes communication burdensome. The parabolic manner of speech finds little acceptance; the preference is for the 'end', the exit so that we can get on with . . . at the expense of exposing the full and deeper meaning of the communication, whether obvious or hidden; the experience becomes onerous, doing no justice to the speaker, the listener's understanding and appreciation stifled. *Communication . . . loses its pleasure. We have become spectators where we once were participants.*

The TV changed much of our source and volume of information. Generally, we read less and watched TV more.

The TV was an entertainment media and it simply put out as many programs that could satisfy viewers. However, the programs once past were past. Only some programs ran again at another time. Conflicts surfaced when we who were more interested in Western movies while Mie and the girls wanted to watch Chinese movies. In short, the availability of programs to all at home required much ordering, and that took time along with compromise, negotiation, and give-and-take gestures. There were some disagreeable moments, and Pa and Mie made sure they held sway in the final decisions. Life returned to normal. It was important that entertainment did not cause disharmony within the family; individually we must continue to be diligent with our primary duties and tasks without slackening or forsaking them. *Discipline must stay its course and run the gauntlet of TV entertainment.*

33

BK on TV

BK was not Burger King which was not in Singapore then. It was Bahasa Kebangsaan the Malay word for national language. At six in the evening, this fifteen minutes lesson would come on the television. It announced the lesson's title and the screen flashed the words individually. One example I remembered well was the word 'pandu'. Just below the English word, 'drive' showed. It would then progress into sentence formation using the key words.

At five minutes before six, I would shout out to some friends who lived a few houses away, to come for Bahasa Kebangsaan and very soon, they gathered, sitting on the floor, in front of the television, with a little notebook just like mine all ready to take notes. Among my friends, Bock Lim was my favourite. See more of him in Endnotes.

BK, our national language was essentially Malay. English was our first language and Chinese our second language. You may think my friends were zealous but truly, they were there more for the cartoon programs that would come on after the BK lesson. I must say that I was the only serious learner of BK as evidenced in all my BK test grades. My friends had little to show for their effort.

At school, BK was not much of an emphasis. Teachers were not particularly in tune with its vision. Students were equally disinterested. So was Chinese. A young and developing nation with eyes set on the international arena focused on an international language, English, to effectively facilitate trade and commerce.

Malay continues to be our national language today. Singapore was in its early history, the land that belonged to the native Malays. The Chinese and Indians were migrants. The government specifically entertained special benefits for the Malay population. BK established this understanding. The effort to propagate BK featured emphatically in our national anthem, yet most of the population other than Malays still cannot pronounce those words nor understand what they mean.

We live in a world of relics.
Symbolism plays its part.
What was the symbol for that relic?
Which relic was for what symbol?
Memory fades, purpose not served.
The symbol stays.

Where there is no vision the people cast off restraint, but blessed is he who keeps the law. Another Bible version says, where there is no vision, the people perish. They mean the same thing. BK was a symbol. Today it is a relic. What will it be tomorrow?

In world history, politics and government initiate policies that often outlive the term of human life such that the affected are not around to witness the intended outcomes. Pa and Mie did not outlive BK and I probably would have passed on before the verdict arrives.

Endnotes

Bock Lim, my favourite friend for BK, lived in the same block as I, two units away on the third floor. Mine was the second floor. We could see each other as we were all in the same long slab block of flats. Our means of communication was by shouting. If I wanted him to attend BK on TV, I shouted "Bock Lim. TV!" His response would be "Coming" or "Later!" if he would miss it. He walked with us to the Thai temple occasionally and worshiped with us. Somehow, he never got around to taking an interest in Buddhism.

He was the eldest son in his family and three other siblings. His father was a carpentry contractor in the shipping trade, sawing and nailing crates, and wooden pallets. His mother was a homemaker. They shared their house with his uncle and his two wives, and six children. Later, Bock Lim's father took another wife. That whole household was the rowdiest between the two blocks that faced each other. They talked loudly and rudely, shouted at each other, the wives threatening their unruly mischievous children who ran up and down their flat, smoking, gambling, and playing truant at school. They went to Jervois East.

When we all grew up, our different interests and aspirations ended our friendship as we saw little of each other. He went to trade school. He married earlier than I did and in due time he took for himself another wife. Their house was much too small for so many and he moved out with his small immediate family. I never saw him again.

When people and circumstance change not,
When mindsets remain unadjusted,
Habits and practices perpetuate.

In Darkness, they saw no Light,
In what was, what is, and what will be . . .
They shall be.

34

Eat More Wheat

We started to see static advertisements flashed on our TV screen about "Eat More Wheat" with a cartoon sketch of a family sitting around the dinner table eating noodles. Another advertisement showed "Eat More Bread" with a bread loaf with part of it sliced and laid flat on a table. Very soon, we saw these similar versions stuck on walls, notice boards, and bus stops all over the island. They appeared everywhere.

I asked Pa what this was all about and he explained that Singapore was into nation building and that bread and noodles came from wheat, which was a lot cheaper than the better staple foodstuffs. The government was suggesting that by eating the cheaper staple every family could then afford to feed more mouths and set aside the saving for supporting a better standard of life. Apparently, wheat has a high composition of protein and energy. It all seemed to make sense.

That drive to "Eat More Wheat" was one of the earliest forms of social engineering the government undertook in its nation-building program: systems engineering in education to health to economics and all things social such as food consumption, family planning, BK and racial harmony, the arts, and culture.

Often, we think we have a problem.
A solution to it we find.
    Done it was.

Then comes along someone wise,
Showed us the problem we thought was,
Really was not.
    Undo we cannot, for done it was.

Let's again look for the real solution
That will take care of the real problem.

Experiments are my thing, but . . . Are not some of these gambles? If they were, the initiators will not live long enough to see how they turn out. We are grateful that for many decades now, 'gambles' have given way to deliberation. We have not yielded to impulse and suggestion; we have taken wise counsel from our betters, not our inclinations; our experiences rigorously considered.

35

Hundred Marks for Chinese

I was in primary three and was in the second term examinations. This incident was during the class Chinese paper. I could answer all the questions except one. It just seemed to slip my mind. There were fifteen minutes left to the bell and I was simply restless about being unable to recall the answer. The girl next to me asked whether I had finished seeing that I had not been writing for some time.

I responded in whispers, "Finished, except for one."

She said, "Which one?"

"Number eleven," I replied.

"I know the answer," she returned.

In a moment of decisive action, I said "Give me the answer and I will give the answer for one question you need to know."

She happily agreed and we 'struck our hands' in a good deal.

I ended with full marks for Chinese a few days later. My girl classmate got her one mark.

I told not one person about the misdemeanour. The girl sitting next to me was the only who knew and we were accomplices to each other. Both of us had no qualms about it. We benefited from it.

Here was a moral test at hand and I failed miserably. What seemed like a 'street-smart' and quick-thinking idea was indeed corrupt in nature. A childish mischief perhaps, yet there was an inherent inclination to such self-centred gain seeking in even a child's nature. The accumulation of such little corruptions builds an addiction to their gains and ultimately to a complete immunity to their error. *For where your treasure is, there will your heart be also.* What a fearful state. How did sin reach us?

Thomas A. Kempis has this to offer:

"For first there cometh to the mind a bare thought of evil, then a strong imagination thereof, afterwards delight and evil motion, then consent."

As for me, I am to this day very ashamed of the incident. It will never go away and stays close to remind, an indelible stain on my conscience. Stay clear of mischief. It haunts our conscience to the grave. My heart reproaches me.

Alas! My Lord Jesus rested the matter: "Go and sin no more."

It was tainted glory!
It was the shame of my life.
I must ever be watchful, ever vigilant;
Temptations forever shun.

All in vain:
The hundred marks are now but nothing.

36

Pa's Toolbox

I t was not really a toolbox but more of a very thick dark green canvas bag. One day Pa returned after work, and brought home a round metal object and was studying it. To further examine the object, he sat down on the floor and tried using some of his basic tools in the lower drawer. He noticed that I was watching the whole episode he called out: "Get the six-spanner."

This put me into an intensive wracking of my brain. Usually Pa would ask for the double-ended spanners, with each end of a different size but never a six-spanner. As I had watched him since the start of this episode, I estimated the sizing and picked up five double-ended ones. I ran to him with all five and he picked the one he needed! I cleared the bar.

In the event above, I feared the rather large tool bag for several reasons: it smelled musty and of rust. Rust covered my hands every time I touched anything in it From time to time Pa would grease the tools, and the grease added to the horrendous smell. The other thing was cockroaches scrambling out when I unzipped it.

Actually a six-spanner was called that simply because it has an 'across flat' that gripped a *hexagonal* (six equal-sided) nut or bolt head to tighten or loosen it. Generally, it was open-ended meaning at both ends but with slightly different sizing so that one piece of spanner served as two spanners. When Pa asked for a six-spanner, I was confused. It was simply 'spanner' as my limited vocabulary allowed. The sizing mattered.

Pa was a quiet person unless agitated. He never had any schooling or formal trade/technical training. All that he learnt was through trial and error. He collected any mechanical stuff that people threw away because they were not able to work them again. For Pa, everything unwanted had a second life. He had a special respect from his colleagues at work. His job title was officially a Fitter. The role he played had mostly been in problem solving.

I learned a fair bit about the different tools, and their use. More than that, I was like an *inexperienced* apprentice who earnestly watched the master at work, not daring to ask, picking up the knowledge through *mental inquiry* as the '*knowledge-full*' master who was at his *experimental inquiry*. It was exhilarating. There was this quiet sense of a meeting of minds when the intended problem was resolved. The low-minded humble apprentice recognised by the wise knowledgeable master, as the father-son relationship developed purposefully.

Humility is lowering one's own esteem, rendering oneself insignificant, inferior, and modest: wherefore bringing willingness to the fore, a willingness to submit to learning. One can learn little when filled with deep-seated predispositions, unjustified preferences, untested ideas, and ungrounded opinions.

More broadly speaking, willingness is about *foregoing any rights* we *inherently own,* and *laying aside any abilities* we can *legitimately lay claim to,* and come to the Master *empty, prepared* for the Master's knowledge. That is humility.

Who can be humble?

Who is so very wise that he knows all things?

Who is so wise that he knows many things, yet ready to listen as though ignorant?

37

Sewage manhole . . . treasure underground

There were a few months in one particular year that Pa seemed to be very busy at work. He would return home every day tired, sweaty and in his work clothes, carrying two little soiled dirty looking sacks and leaving them in the bathroom. Pa told Mie that all of a sudden, the PWD (Public Works Department) had several sewerage projects and summoned Pa to visit the various sites daily. Overtime would be heavy in the next several months. Mie put us all on alert so that we prepared not to get in Pa's way, not to agitate him, and not to create trouble. We would help when called upon.

One day Pa returned early and went to work on his soiled bags. I watched him outside the bathroom while he opened up the bags, which were full with coins, dirty looking, with much scum all over. Pa had another bag of sand and he grabbed some sand to rub against the coins. I picked up enough courage to ask where the coins came from and why they were so poorly looking. Pa explained that while he was down in the drainage manholes to investigate some trouble with chokes and blockages, he found the coins. Most of the coins were usable, some were of times past, and he could not tell until he

103

had them washed. I offered my help and Pa assigned me to rubbing the coins with sand until they were reasonably visible.

There were so many things in the drainage manholes. The manholes were circular holes constructed in the ground at intervals along the huge underground drainage pipe that carried sewerage and wastewater from the houses to the wastewater treatment plant. They provided access to check blockages and condition of the system.

The multitude of coins was quite a find. It was a treasure and aptly a pot of gold in the hideous sewers. How they got there was a puzzle. Human excreta and wastewater passed through these sewers, the coins were not likely to be from the excreta; they were likely to be washed into the sewers along with wastewater. Pa never expected this and never knew how much they would add up to. They were mostly small coins: one-cent and five-cent, and some bronze ones with the head of Queen Victoria on them.

Pa washed the coins and laid them out on an old absorbent rag to soak up the water. He then stacked them in columns of fifty coins and rolled them into pieces of paper he had cut to size earlier on. Each roll represented fifty one-cent or fifty five-cent coins. He wrote '1-cent' or '5-cent' on side of each roll. The rolls are set against each other to ensure that they are not short of or more by a coin. Those other odd sizes went into little plastic bags, each containing a slip of paper showing the value therein.

This was not a one-off activity as in that whole month Pa brought bag one or two bags at least twice weekly. It was a time of absolute focus on getting the coins ready for the bank tellers and collecting the fruits of the effort. Pa washed the coins with fine sand, then with detergent, dried, counted, and collated them in rolls for ultimate despatch to the bank. It was not a fortune but worthy of the effort.

Fruits are available in their due season. However, the tree needed diligent tending. Effort produces fruits. Loving and careful effort produces sweet and delightful fruits. *We reap what we sow . . .*

Effort requires care: fine sand cleaned the coins gently so that the images on them are visibly intact and acceptable as legal tender. They are organised and stacked in rolls of fifty coins so as not to inconvenience the bank tellers' work: they would be happier for it.

Pa saw the value in coins in the scum. He also saw the hard work to clean them in order to collect their true value. Pa had always been such: *he saw a second life in things unwanted and cast away. He made us see great value in the lowly, in the rejected.*

Wealth gotten *by vanity shall be diminished: but he that gathers by labour shall increase.*

38

Daily News . . . Friday Background

T he television became quite an important aspect of our lives. News from the TV was a flourish. We sat around together to watch the news daily, and on Friday there was a news round-up programme that provided special reporting, analysis, and commentary for the goings-on in the world. We would never miss the news. News became an inseparable part of our lives and we watched it daily with a compulsion like it was our daily bread. The 6.30pm quick news and the nine o'clock full news coverage became our staple.

Pa would pick up English and now had content on things around him, new knowledge, new meaning, that exposed the happenings about him. It became a big thing and was all-good for us children and for Pa.

Pa had a different and I might say a slanted view about politics. It was common for poorer and older folks to gather at coffee shops in the early evening to talk about news they picked up from the newspapers or from friends or colleagues at the workplace. People reported, threw in their opinions, complained, and cited exceptional examples as representative of the truth about what someone did, why he did or should not have, or how the government had badly performed. The coffee shop was a place that such people congregate to exhibit their idleness, vent their frustrations and disillusionment about life, and forward their *generalisations* about anything under the sun.

Watching the TV news particularly the local news, was much like a coffee shop except the people were we the young children. We did not understand much about politics and government. We were just happy carefree children and found it hard to understand the angst and rising anger in Pa whenever the state implemented some sweeping national policies or when the prime minister was filmed visiting a poor home and the like. Pa proclaimed it as propaganda and discounted the policies to manipulation for political gains.

———◆⋙◆———

We could sense the animosity in Pa about local politics, a deep-seated unhappiness that had festered into a rage. On many occasions we had questions to which we had few clear answers; the rage smothered all inquiry. Usually, the end was *unhappy. I thought I caught view of happiness from unhappiness during these moments.* A happy thing is a happy thing if enjoyed as it is. A happy thing becomes unhappy when thrown at with unexplainable opinions and unreasonable positions.

There was certainly a huge divide in Pa's and our views of life whenever politics entered the news; it was as mud slung at the face of happiness. We were at opposite poles. We were a young nation and we had too many unanswered questions, Pa was not of much help with unmoveable, solidly anchored preconceived notions that failed often to make sense to us. We refrained from too many questions to not fuel rage. *No major local political news on TV was good news.* They may be misreports, untruth, misplaced opinions, and fuel much unneeded vexations.

It would be well to shun discussions of worldly affairs, in this case politics and government, as they are unnecessary distractions and a vexation to the spirit. Such discussions end up with no actionable outcome, just all talk. Not enough deep thinking goes into them, few facts if any, enter into them. One ends up all twisted with anger and disillusionment. Passions breed unrest.

39

Weekend TV Movies

On the weekends, we watched the late night movies and were acquainted with Westerns starring John Wayne, serials like Lone Ranger, Ponderosa, Laramie, Lassie, Ben Casey, and Dr. Kildare. We watched the amazing Shirley Temple whenever there was a movie featuring her. These were like two-hour long movies and usually ended past midnight. Mie and the girls watched Chinese mostly Cantonese and Taiwanese movies in the early evening hours.

Chinese movies oftentimes were 'sob' stories where a young lover was jilted, or some wrong done to an innocent person that was righted only years later highlighting the hand of destiny; good always won over evil, young women being bullied and abused and by sheer grit how they received just reprisal. They portrayed how the downtrodden poor became successful in restitution of earlier wicked treatments from more powerful bullies. Mie and the girls would shed tears over them. Occasionally, we boys watched these movies until we were bored with them. In fact, we were able to predict the outcomes most of the time. There was an underlying theme of *karma* at work, the inevitable cosmic law of 'good begets good, and evil, evil'.

Western stories were about cowboys and red Indians, shootouts, a sheriff going after a murderer or a bank robber. John Wayne was always the good person. He never ever acted as a bad person. Occasionally, we might have a Roman gladiator or Grecian warrior with shield and spear. We got a little of popular history without ever knowing its accuracy or authenticity. There were also modern movies of which I particularly loved to watch the young sweet-talking Shirley Temple. That was her role: cute sweet-talker, smiling and full of charm, able to sing, dance, and entertain. Whether it was Western or Chinese movies, they were about good winning over bad, the righteous over the wicked.

———— ✧ ————

Chinese movies were *emotional* and tended to cast characters in clear-cut specific roles of villain and the righteous. The themes were as mentioned above—traditional and oriental. Western movies carried all the American culture of embracing and kissing even as a greeting, the manner of speaking was straight, fast, and full of confidence—*liberal and open*—all very visibly *physical*.

My observation was that Chinese movies tended to *drag*, heighten, and *stretch* the process from maltreatment or affliction, through the suffering, and out of it to restitution. The extent was a strong thematic suggestion and naturally, an infusion of it in the audience's mind through pitiful 'sob' for the victim and rage against the abuser. 'Right' came about passively as destined by the heavens. In its due season, 'Wrong' turned around or set right.

English movies were more direct, the process of pain *shortened* as though it was obvious, leading quickly to the intended end. The centre stage provided much action and activity to portray villainy and the heroism that caused the favourable outcomes.

Endnotes

In business today, in an adaptation of the western culture, we often hear this: 'I do not care how it is to be done, just get it done'. There is a certain impatience for results. A Chinese might say, 'if you want quick sprouts, cast beans; if you want profits, grow oaks'. Yes, the beans sprout in a few days and sold cheaply with little profit, the oak obviously economically useful and highly profitable only in tens of years when the wood is ready to harvest.

Grandma and Aunt, notice they both wore the sarong
kebaya, dressing of the Babas and Nonyas.

40

Aunt Meets Uncle Bah

A unt was a very distant relative on my grandma's side in Penang, something too complex for me to understand. She was close to our family and stayed with us for many years in a room together with GGA. They applied to the state for the one-room flat at the adjacent eighteen-storey flats where the grazing field for cows and goats once were. They moved when the application was successful.

Uncle Bah, totally unknown to Aunt, was another one of those visitors from Penang, someone related to someone who knows my grandma. He was alone, no wife, no child, in his early fifties. He spoke with reasonably good English, carrying the unmistakable accent of the Penang people who visited us perennially. Well educated, he works at the former British Administration. Pa told us he was from a wealthy family but had not made good with his inheritance. He was particularly loud and agitated when he spoke. The loud expression demanded a dominance that trampled over all other voices. He likes to carry a handkerchief to clean the sweat off his forehead and wipe his mouth, almost like a trademark. Uncle Bah was simply queer, idiosyncratic, lived in his own world, unconcerned with issues of life, read the daily newspapers as though he read every word, enjoyed

113

showing his 'magic' tricks to us young ones, and drawing attention unto himself.

Uncle Bah attracted us much because he had an almost endless repertoire of tricks to bedazzle us; we were amazed and awestruck without end. In those after-dinner evenings before the time of TV, we would gather in front him as he performed his tricks. He folded a one-dollar currency note, in very sharp folding actions until it became a little rectangle of folds. He had one of us to blow into the folded note before he unfolded it. It turned out to be a plain piece of white paper: the dollar note had become a blank piece of paper! How did he do it? Where did the dollar note go? To all of these questions, Uncle Bah had a solution: bring back the dollar note, and he did. He folded the blank piece of paper, had one of us blow into it, unfolded it again, and presto, a dollar note appeared before our very eyes! He laughed with great pleasure whenever we were amazed. It was his victory.

He had so many tricks in his repertoire, with coins, cards, eggs, newspapers, handkerchief, and so on. He does a trick and at the most two every evening and kept us coming back for more.

Grandma had visitors almost all the year round, from her Penang birthplace. It appears as though every one of them is a relative of some sort. Aunt had married a rich Teochew (Chinese dialect) man and raised a son and two daughters. Her husband divorced her and took the children. Our house was a kind of mini-hotel that was able to accommodate an additional two at any one time. In such situations, the living hall became a temporary bedroom in the evening. Uncle Bah used a foldable canvas stretcher bed to sleep in at night. In the morning he folded it and kept it away neatly in grandma's room.

Aunt stayed some years with us before Uncle Bah came on the scene. They became a pair sometime later, and started with passing chats, developing into a liking, and ended with taking walks in the evening. Then they decided to live together. We heard that Uncle Bah went back to Penang and died there. Aunt lived alone until her death, GGA died earlier on.

As far as the East was from the West, Aunt and Uncle Bah were just that. How they came to be a pair was beyond us. I can only imagine that *companionship was their crying need*, and as long as there was willingness to bare that need, there was a meeting of minds in spite of their individual peculiarities.

Aunt, Uncle Bah, GGA and grandma alike, up until their very last breaths, lived unfulfilled lives. They took whatever came, irresolute about what to do about their lives, and by the time they did arrive at any idea many things were not there or had worked against them. They lived unto themselves and saw little beyond that despite the loneliness.

Time faithfully rolls *on* all that *we want*: joy, bliss, gladness, delight, peace, contentment . . . an unfilled cup of goodness.

When Time faithfully rolls *off,* all *we get* are pain, suffering, distress, grief, misery, sorrow, despair, adversity, vexation, wastefulness, recklessness, desperation, loneliness, depression, emptiness . . . a full cup of woes.

Time is neutral. *What is broken?* Perhaps the means to getting what we want decide what we get. In the law of nature, that is cause and effect. Beyond the means, there is another hand at work that we have simply not taken time to recognise.

Human beings cannot live unto themselves. What keeps us all ticking is meaning and purpose, found only in relation to others. That requires a fellowship, a bond, and communication to thrive. *Companionship* is fellowship, a union with another or others, bonded by the language of loving care and caring love.

41

Mie's amah career

When we were a little older, Mie began to explore becoming a stay-out amah to supplement the family income that was solely borne by Pa. Our growing family would benefit from it. Mie had a close younger friend who was an amah and she introduced Mie to it. All she needed was to be able to greet the employer and converse on essentials, in English. Her first was as amah to an English military family. Her friend who worked for such English families introduced an employer and Mie got started. She fared reasonably well as the tasks were essentially menial: cleaning/tidying, laundry, changing curtains, some cooking, and washing. As very little two-way communication was required, the little English in her vocabulary was adequate. Mostly the employer directed what wanted done.

These English families were couples without children. Some had children, which was more challenging. Their children were always 'wild' and did things that were dangerous or could be dangerous, in which case when they got into trouble, they hurt and cry, and got over them quickly. They were back on them again and learnt quickly to avoid the same trouble. I must say they were fun to play with on those occasions when Mie took me with her during the school holidays.

The compensation of an amah was acceptably equitable for the effort applied and at the qualifications expected. Mie learnt that having letters of commendation or referral was a good practice. She learnt this from her friend. Mie collected such letters from all her employers. They spoke much about her ability and conduct and became instrumental in her subsequent applications for such employment.

The income was half of what Pa made and weighed much in the family's overall sustenance. Mie had to pay Dajie, our domestic helper about a fifth of her takings. All considered, it was an agreeable career that kept things running as they had been, in that we children need not suffer neglect.

A *good* name *is* rather to be chosen than great riches, *and* loving favour rather than silver and gold.

42

The Papworths

O f all of Mie's employers, I remembered the Papworths best probably because Mie worked the longest for them and I had the most interaction with their son David who was about my age but bigger in size. The man of the house was Ian, the wife Ann, son David, and daughter Gillian. Ian was a staff sergeant in the Royal Air Force at Tengah Airbase. The wife and children were involved with the Boy Scouts and Girl Guides. They were very smart looking whenever I visited on Saturdays.

David had regular magazines on Beano, a cartoon series, and I read about Big Dan the fumbling cartoon character. In those newsprint magazines, they covered news from England, quizzes, general knowledge snippets, puzzles, history of famous people, and the like. I enjoyed these magazines very much. David treasured them and we both spent much time on the puzzles. He was sometimes cheeky and bullied me a little. I always took it in good spirit and we continued to enjoy the things in common.

With Mr. and Mrs. Papworth, my communications were normally brief and with a smile. Sometimes it was difficult to decipher their heavy English accents.

They had taken a liking to Singapore curry and on Chinese New Year's Day Mie invited them over to our home for lunch. Pa would busy himself in cooking the chicken and beef curry along with some Chinese fares.

The Papworths were in Singapore for a short time and transferred home to England when Mr. Papworth's term was up. Mie kept in touch with Mrs. Papworth through Christmas and New Year cards. I handled the writing, enquiring about their well-being and the usual courtesies. One day, Mrs. Papworth wrote to say she and her husband had divorced. He had an affair with a friend of hers. We wrote to express our sadness over the matter and that was the last we heard from her.

It was sad that the happy family we knew them to be had now broken up. I was puzzled but did not understand or thought much about it. The father of one of my neighbourhood friends took a second wife but the first wife continued to live together. They got along pretty well and lived like a family. There was no departure of the first wife from that house.

Families are just that. Geographic differences usually mean differences in culture, in language, in practices. I saw the Papworths as seemingly happy people, their attitudes were more easy-going, and they never quarrelled.

From my interactions with David, I learnt that they had a lot more information and access to knowledge that I do not have, be they general or English-specific in nature.

Seemingly, contented and good people can in their lust, become perverted. True peace of heart rests in resisting passions not in feeding, and satisfying them. God's standard is not to look upon a woman to lust after her, in so doing one has committed adultery. Adultery is sin. What a sure standard, yet the eyes of man open him to lustful distractions, temptations, and to sin. God's standard sets the mark. The flesh is weak but the spirit is willing; the spirit did not separate from the flesh hence the will wallow in the flesh, and missed the mark.

It is worth a reminder from Thomas A, Kempis: *"For first there cometh to the mind a bare thought of evil, then a strong imagination thereof, afterwards delight and evil motion, then consent."*

Lust not after her beauty in thine heart; neither let her take thee with her eyelids.

43

Our domestic helper

She lived in the Bukit Ho Swee/ Henderson vicinity and was a day helper with us children as Mie took up a career as amah to British military families stationed in Singapore. We all addressed our helper as elder sister Dajie. She spoke to us in Fujian, her voice slightly nasal, her build stocky but not short in proportion. Through a few physical struggles with her, I discovered she was strong, too strong for me. She never hesitated to use the cane whenever necessary. I liked her, very straightforward and predictable. She could enjoy a good laugh with us.

———◈———

Dajie came from a poor family in the Henderson Kampong. Her siblings were many but not more than our family's. She left schooling early and was in her very early twenties old enough to supervise us the young ones. We tended to be cheeky and tested how far we could stretch the liberty we now had in the absence of Mie, who had embarked on the amah career.

When we were away at school, she would do the basic marketing for the day, clear the laundry, and put them out to dry before we returned from school. Our porridge would be ready when we reached home, she made sure we had our shower, settled down to do our homework, and played at home until the late afternoon, while she continued with other household chores. She would leave for her home once Mie came back from work.

We never could go past the bounds Mie have laid for us. There appeared to be a conspiracy between Mie and Dajie that kept us out of any prospective adventures beyond the established bounds.

She was like Mie in her handling of us. She was many years older than Bao Yu my oldest sister. Dajie ruled with a strong hand physically and by virtue of her position in the household.

She was a wonderful helper, more like the oldest of us all, and like a super sister. She understood from her own dim circumstances what it meant to work outside of her own home, how to deal with mischievous boys as us, and how to interact with all types of people. She was tough and kind. She identified our mischief instinctively and we never could outsmart her.

44

Roving food vendors

I n our vicinity, there were four blocks of flats, with each having twenty-four families. Roving hawkers or food vendors were a common sight. They come around in a large three-wheeler in the case of Soya sauce, a bicycle with a large box that opens out at the back into a table in the case of the Bread man. The Satay man had his two organised stalls for the stove and store. The sesame dough (Mua Chee) man danced to his cutting and mixing actions of the dough. The 'bean pearl' (Tau Suan) man had some tiny squat stools hooked around one stall for customers who sat around it for a quick bowl of 'tau suan' soup. It was not really soup but starch added to yellow split beans soup to achieve a clear sticky solution making the beans stay in place looking like yellow pearls. Roasted chestnuts were also popular in those days. These were the small portable types of vendor stalls where slow cooking, low fire, and simple food handling were required.

The Char Kway Teow (fried noodles) vendor was quite a different story. She had a larger pushcart that had a very large and deep frying pan in the centre, with a charcoal stove just below to fire up the frying pan. Her sauces in glass bottles were in a long half height box at the side. Her kway teow (wide and white noodles) and yellow noodles were in plastic bags in another box compartment. The customer may ask for the kway teow to contain egg or be without egg. She was the only vendor who plied her trade on the streets because of the big fire and larger stall size. She charged thirty cents for char kway teow without egg.

———✧———

These roving vendors were rather creative in the manner they built their food stalls on their transport mode. They were highly adaptive. The bread man had his box strapped to the pillion space at the back of his bicycle, the back of box opening outwards when unlatched to serve as a bread-cutting or slicing worktable. The unsliced fresh loaves went to the top of the box to serve as store for extra supplies. To make his arrival known he pressed his vehicle horn and shouted out 'Roti' in a sonorous voice as though singing. Roti is bread in Malay.

The Satay Man sold satay—chicken, beef, or mutton seasoned and skewered on thin 'lili' sticks—and ketupat, rice compressed and wrapped in woven green palm leaves like a dumpling, strung together and boiled. The satay man was usually Malay and had no pork satay. Malays were Muslims and shunned pork for religious reasons. He carried two identical separate stalls hung at each end of a large halved-bamboo pole over his shoulder. One stall was for the charcoal supply and fire to roast the satay, the other was for the sauce, the uncooked satay, ketupat, and packing bags. He used a handheld fan to fan the flames of the stove.

The Soy sauce vendor had a cartful of different types of soya sauces: light, dark, thick dark. The grades were ordinary, medium, and high quality. He sold vinegar, the white and black types. There also sold preserved vegetables in large earthen pots, salt, pepper, monosodium glutamate. If I classify him now, he was a seasoning vendor but his main business was in soya sauces.

The Indian peanuts vendor came on the scene shouting 'kacang putih' with a low height box resting on the towel like turban of his head. He carried a foldable cross-stand to hold the box when he chose to stop temporarily to sell the nuts. He had a small variety of six to eight types of nuts. 'Kacang putih' is Malay for white nuts, simply de-skinned shelled peanuts coated with a light layer of white sugar. The buyers, mostly children would approach him for what they wanted, and he would take a long thin cone into which he would deftly pick up a palm full of the nuts and slid them using his other hand. The cones were used exercise book pages rolled tightly and secured by folding in the tip.

As a drummer would rattle the cowbell about his drum set, the Fujian prawn noodle assistant ran about the street with a cut section of the bamboo as a surface to rattle a thin strip of similar bamboo against it, producing a sonorous medium-pitched sound to herald 'Hokkien Mee', all ready to take orders. Some people called the vendor the 'tock-tock mee'.

These vendors were smart business people who balanced the manner of conducting their businesses from the small to not so small. Their prices charged, time taken to prepare the food, types of food sold (perishable), value of the food ingredients, fuel cost, how they plied their trade—on the street or within the flats of residences—figured into their business plans.

Their marketing was mostly by shouting out, announcing, and proclaiming their presence. Retention of their business was service familiarity, convenience, and quality. The only competition was alternative or substitute food, that is, between satay, tausuan, and muachee and so on. For each particular food, only one vendor for each food type existed: one for Char Kway Teow, one for Satay, one for Soy sauce, and so on. The small market required them to differentiate by quality, trust, neighbourliness, and friendship.

Endnotes

Roving vendors included the Indian barber Muthu. He would provide haircuts to Pa, Cai, and I. Muthu would work, save, and send money to his family in India. He was a tall fellow, always in white short-sleeved shirts and dark pants. He carried a black brief case the size of a foot and half by a foot. In it are his manual cutters, scissors, shavers, a small handheld mirror, cologne, powder, and water spray. He walked around the blocks of flats and carried a large umbrella to shelter from the sun and rain.

Mie's sister-in-law, a hairdresser did better. Whenever she was about on call, she had many heads to work with—Mie, Yu, Zhu, Lian, Zuan, and the neighbours. In those days, vendors came to our doorsteps literally. Today we go to hairdressing salons, provision shops, minimarts, supermarkets, and hypermarkets. What had happened? Bigger markets meant more consumers, their mobility, improved supply economics, standard of living, growth in variety, and others played their hands to precipitate the change.

45

Empty going down . . . Full coming up . . .

The block of flats, where our house was on the second floor was 3-storied. Every time the roving food vendors called between our block and the next, the residents who wanted to buy any food would shout out to the vendor what they wanted. The vendor would go on to prepare the order. Sometimes, it were cooked food like satay (pork, chicken, beef, or mutton on sticks) which had to be roasted over fire, the residents on the upper floors would lower down the tiffin or containers in a basket for the vendor to use. Once the food is cooked, the residents would once again lower the basket with the appropriate payment. The vendor collected his payment and placed the food in the basket and the residents pulled them up. Where bread was concerned, this was one way of handling the order if the buyer wanted loose bread with kaya-spread. However, the bread man resorted to throwing the plain bread packed in a plastic bag, because the bread was soft and light, there was nothing like kaya that could mess up the bread.

Kaya is soft and more fluid than peanut butter. It is a cooked mix of eggs, sugar, flavouring, coconut, and pandan leaf to provide the fragrance.

The flats were three-storied making this mode of lowering and pulling up a basket viable. The cooked food vendor had a practice of chatting with their customers on the second to third storey while the food is cooking. It was a friendly customer-vendor relationship.

What goes up must come down: the natural law of gravity.

What is empty going down must be full when coming up: positive hope in things unseen, in things yet to be.

Life is empty when things are down, full when things look up: emotion in response to things seen, to things that are now here. Whatever be, these cyclical things and events come and go. Despair and Hope are life's just fare.

46

Hot Tea for All

Our favourite drink was tea. I had not noticed a brand but it had the picture of a cock on a globe on a loose red wrapper that wrapped round the tealeaves packed in silvery foil. That packet was for twenty cents, like a brick but a tiny one of 2 inches long by 1 inch wide and 1 inch high. The tea was strong enough to fill the aluminium tiffin container, enough for six small mugs. It was easy to prepare, boil a kettle full of water, release a packet of tealeaves into the aluminium tiffin container, pour in the boiled water, and cover the tiffin container to let the tea brew. After a while, open the cover and the fragrance of tea comes off strong, the colour a rich orange-red, and the leaves all expanded rise to the surface, it is time to add some sugar, and stir it a little. Cover the tiffin container for five minutes. Remove the tealeaves with a fine handheld sieve. The tea is ready for drinking.

We usually took tea after dinner. On the weekends, we might have one in the afternoon and took it with Marie biscuits. If one tiffin container was not enough we brewed another. We all loved and enjoyed tea immensely, its fragrance, its strong aroma, its feel in the mouth . . . it was something we could all help in making.

Tea was nice. The packets we bought came with the right size so we did not have to purchase large quantities or store them. We went out to the provision store and bought off the shelf when needed we it. It was cheap. It was easy to prepare, a packet enough to make a tiffin container of 'perfect' tea of the right strength, the right aroma, colour, and taste.

We always drank our tea black and mildly sweetened. We never had to drink tea alone; there was always someone to share it.

We do not sit around to have tea as the aristocratic Englanders; we took our cuppa and drank it in front of the TV, at our study desks, and anywhere at home. Tea was for us a family thing, not a private entertainment of sort. It was second to the water Mie boiled twice daily, and cooled in empty Johnnie Walker whisky bottles for our drinking needs. Water was the best drink for the body, tea the best drink for the family.

47

Court-less Badminton

The badminton court we played at was an imaginary one. It included a walk path made of concrete tiles that led all the way to the end of the block. Dry earth was on all sides with some parts covered with scant bits of grass. The 'court' was not usable after a rain.

———◆———

The ground on which we played badminton was uneven with raised concrete tiles, a covered manhole, earth and grass patches. It was an imagined court: its length was the walk path from the drain to the manhole. Its breadth was between the laundry rack posts of the two houses facing each other. There were no double lines at the side and back of the *imagined court* as there were in a real court. There were also no short-served lines at the front.

For the *net*, we did not have one. We pulled a pink raffia string between the laundry posts to serve as the top of the net.

Our *racquets* were used ones. One that I had was from my youngest uncle. It was an old Dunlop with a rusty metal stem. The leather grip was still good. The strings were in disrepair but we had learned to restring it. We had another wooden racquet that though newer had loose strings.

The cork *shuttlecocks* were used ones but still offered reasonable strike and flight.

Next was the important element that we had no control over. This is an imaginary open court subjected to the *natural wind*. When it was windless we had great games, gentle breezes were workable. Strong and irregular blowing winds made it sensible for us to leave the game.

The imaginary court and all the subnormal conditions and equipment made Cai and I reasonably good players. We trained against the natural elements. Cai became a school player in college. I pursued another activity altogether.

Endnotes

The less favourable conditions made us good players. They stretched us physically and raised our skills level. They raised the bar for us to deal with unusual behaviours of the flight of a shot from the opponent due to shuttlecock inconsistency, a sleight of the wind, a slip off the concrete walk path, a broken racquet string, and so on.

Life is much like that. One does not always have the conditions wished. There is often a need to adapt and make good with what is given. At the end, one is better for it having received training in the school of hard knocks, refined in the furnace, established in the storms of life. As fire tempers iron, so the court-less badminton conditions our skills and nimbleness.

Compare with athletic, sport, and gymnastics training in China, Russia, Korea . . . where methods and the physical body are put through the most intense and difficult simulations to get them to optimise and maximise strength, stamina, flexibility, and balance. Afflictions help improve performance.

48

Roving Provision ' Shop '

We bought all our regular provisions such as rice, sugar, cooking oil, soap, detergent and the like from a provision shopkeeper who had his shop at a location many miles from our house. He would be on his bicycle with our previous order delivered to our doorstep. He then collected what was outstanding from the last delivery, usually half the bill value, and collected half the value of the current delivery. We therefore had a credit term of half a month. Our shopkeeper's nickname was 'Siow' meaning crazy in Fujian. He was Hainanese (another Chinese dialect group from Hainan Island in southern China) and muscular at the shoulders from hefting rice bags and provisions. Behind his bicycle, he had a sturdy box strapped to the bicycle frame with used internal air tubing of the bicycle tyre.

Pa would complain that his prices were higher, and he would brush it off with comments that he was giving better quality, the door-to-door delivery and credit terms. He was often persuasive, laughing it off and sharing news and jokes. He was always willing to laugh off the brunt of adverse or harsh comments.

Siow would not be able to do a viable business by tending to his shop waiting for walk-in customers. He resorted to this method of a roving provision shop while his wife attended to the shop, and he was out delivering and soliciting new business. With the bicycle, he could handle one delivery per trip.

He did well and soon owned a delivery van to deliver customer orders. This enabled him to deliver several orders at one drive.

The delivery van eventually became a roving store with additional items other than the delivery orders. He could easily pass them off as cash sales to casual customers on his route or replenished their stocks.

Siow was willing and diligent in survival, and growth was his reward. He was creative in seeking growth, and business development was his reward. One led to another.

49

Tearful Chilli Pounding

From our early years, we got used to eating hot and spicy curry because our nonya grandma was our household's matriarch and curry was nearly her staple. We grew to love curry and had it every Saturday and Sunday. As we grew older, we became involved with pre-cooking preparations. There was a process to it all. First, there were the garlic and shallots whose skins required peeling—this was easy. Thinly slicing the bulb of lemon grass and cutting the leaves to shorter lengths were next. We then pounded them together with dried chill in a shallow granite mortar. This was the tough part. My initial attempts proved me a novice, the items in the shallow mortar kept rising up around the sides, and I had to use a spoon to hold them down. It took fifteen minutes to pound the ingredients to an even pulp. Up to this stage, I sniffed and was teary from the spicy, stinging, and fiery waft of the mix of garlic, shallots, and chilli. Some chilli pulp had spluttered onto my white singlet. It was messy. I improved over time and became quite proficient no longer having to beg to pound chilli, Mie or Pa requested my service.

Belacan, a mildly hardened prawn paste rolled around the tip of a butter-knife, slid into a low burning fire, and turned over every minute until a tempting prawn aroma filled the air. That signalled the time to pound it with the pulp mixture of garlic, shallots, lemon grass, and chilli.

Earlier on, we had fresh coconut, broken in pieces, and grated. The next process was to squeeze the milk out of the grated coconut, through a fine sieve. With some water added to the coconut pulp, we squeezed further until milked.

In the meanwhile, Mie heated the earthen pot over the fire, scooped some cooking oil with a large spoon, and put it into the heated pot. Some mixed chilli pulp went in next, followed by some coconut milk, and evenly mixed. This went on until all the chilli and coconut milk were all in the pot. By then the pot had heated up to maximum, and the tempting curry flavour sent those in the living hall into the kitchen to catch its fragrance. The meat, usually chicken or beef, separately seasoned with curry powder went into the pot earlier on as it was heating up. When cooked, we took the fire down to slow burning.

What mattered most to me was the distinctive taste and flavour of curry gravy, it was not thick but strong enough to whet the appetite. With just the gravy, I could eat several plates of plain rice. The chicken or beef in the curry was nice to have but was not the primary thing, the curry gravy was. Pounding the chilli and shedding tears over it, was all worthwhile.

Whenever willing, we can learn new skills. Chilli pounding was such a skill. However, when the learning gets tough the doing must continue with added vigour. It is through the doing that we get to the learning. By doing joyfully, we begin to understand how to not 'fight' the elements but instead to work with them and lighten the process.

We begin to understand the properties of every component in the chilli pulp: the dried chilli, the garlic, the shallots, nutmeg, lemon grass, and so on. We begin to know what goes in first, what next. *They are varied. Just like people, we have tall and short, fat and thin, witty and dull, quiet and talkative, lazy and diligent, bashful and brash. They have to blend well.* Get the process in order, they will fit and harmonise.

We appreciate that pounding is not about dropping the same pounder and weight on every item in the mortar. *They require careful attention to bring out their best qualities: texture, flavour, colour, taste, fragrance.* Pay careful attention to their individuality, their individual uniqueness.

50

Daily Swill Collection

S will was a big thing in those days, at least it was for the swill collectors. They drove miles around in their pick-up trucks, holding up three large round metal drums, and about twenty half-foot square tins with the top cut out, having holes on opposite sides near the top to put in thick bent wire handles. They would park at the roadside and bring up the empty tins to the houses in my block of flats to exchange the filled swill tins from the day before for the empty ones. It was hard work removing the filled tins, as the collector had to carry two from the third floor, pick up two more from the second floor, and two from the ground floor, and all the way to the truck. Then he did the same for the next pair of houses. Every block had twelve pairs or twenty-four houses. There were four blocks on our stretch.

The collectors were actually farmers. The swill was food for the pigs that they bred. The pigs were an important source of income when they grow to the right size for slaughter. The farmers were collecting free swill that would cost them nothing except for removing them from the houses and transporting them back to their farms. This happened every day, rain or shine.

We did not have to give the collectors the swill but they were glad to service us. As an incentive for us to use their free service, they occasionally gave us some eggs from their farm. We could have cleared our swills in plastic bags, tie them up, and let them down the rubbish chute. That would bring up the stench from the chute each time we opened it to discard 'rubbish'. It was a good service the swill collectors provided, and no one had any reason to turn them away.

<hr>

The healthy and fair collaboration made life convenient and bearable for the dwellers, and allowed the farmers a ready supply of swill all year round in exchange for some eggs. Swill collection came to a natural death as pig farms resettled in the government's land use planning, and pig farming became centralised. The changing landscape was also a factor, modern methods of pig farming meant the type of swill was not in use. Pigs now consume processed feed.

What I missed was the sight of diligent swill collectors doing their rounds. My aunt, Mie's oldest sister who lived in the Henderson/Redhill kampong reared pigs, and their resettlement to HDB flats ended their livelihood and their farming lives. They received compensation from the authorities and made some difficult adjustments from living on a farm with wide-open spaces, usefully occupied in pig farming, rearing chickens, growing vegetables as food, and as supplemental income. With the resettlement, they lived in small flats of concrete walls, of many storeys, gave up a life and lifestyle they have been accustomed to for much of their lives. The active life on a farm was gone and my aunt ended up with several illnesses that she would probably never have had living on a farm. She died bed-ridden from issues of the heart and diabetes.

Resettlement became a dislocation for many. Modernisation in its march driven on its own steam saw no stopping. The sacrifice of some had to make way for the vision of the many . . . Life is after all not *what we live in*: a small walled concrete flat with all the convenient amenities or wooden kampong shacks in large, wide, open spaces or a palatial bungalow by the shoreline. It is about *what we look for*, surely not in educational attainments, social and economic achievements in the modern sphere; it is for the purpose, the aim, the direction to live to a meaningful end.

Lives are lived and led . . . by others. Are we ever free to live our lives? Physically, materially, we are under authority, under law. What is freedom?

Freedom is what we can give to the things of God with the same acuteness that other men give to worldly affairs. We must first know and believe in God in order to know the things of God. We must have an ardent fervour to pursue and work in His will.

51

Longest string of firecrackers

The open field next to our blocks of flats which earlier on was used by the grazing cows and goats was eventually used by the authority to build several eighteen-storey flats. They had flats facing each other along a long common corridor. In those days, these were by far the tallest I had seen.

One Chinese New Year's eve, the residents hung a line of firecrackers from the topmost floor all the way to the ground and set it off. The firecrackers' deafening din crackled on, non-stop; it was quite a remarkable sight, excitement was in the air. When it was all over sometime after midnight, the road in front was a sea of red paper from the exploded crackers.

It was traditional Chinese belief that the long string of firecrackers was like a long fiery dragon that continued to crackle with strength on the eve to usher in the New Year. This boded well for business and every other blessing for the people who sponsored the event. It was a great backdrop to ushering in the auspicious Chinese New Year.

———◆———

This event was an awesome novelty for all of us. We had never seen anything that long and sustaining. In fact, it was a surprise to most of us and mid way through some of us wondered when it would end. This traditional practice is no longer with us today and Chinese New Year is not quite the same. It is more tamed and less rowdy. Other fundamental practices around it that remain are the red packets, oranges, reunion dinner, visitations, and so on. Firecrackers have disappeared as they were a fire hazard when Singapore grew up and became more densely populated, a changing of the times. With it, the frequency of *accidental* fires became miniscule. They made way for progress. Streets are not untidy and strewn with shreds of exploded crackers. The 'red' of Chinese New Year symbolising good fortune still stays with us in the red packets of money doled out from elders to the younger ones, in the decorations, and the like; the rowdiness gone except for the humdrum lion dances and the occasional 'washing' or mixing of mahjong card tablets to while away the festive time.

52

Pasar Malam (night bazaar)

Pasar (Malay for market) malam (Malay for night) was a night bazaar where vendors displayed their goods on wooden trays or large plastic sheets on the roadside on the inside of the road kerb. Each stall had its own lamp mostly flamed ones. They sold cloth, clothes for all ages and sexes, sandals, fake leather or polyvinyl wallets and handbags, nail cutters, scissors, tools, unbranded watches, bracelets, raincoats, umbrellas, used comic books, old magazines and books, and very much the things you find in a flea market.

For lighting, some used improvised acetylene lamps, mantle lamps or kerosene lamps. The mantle lamps were brightest and produced very consistent white light, it required the stall owner to initiate a 'pumping' action to bring fuel from the base of the lamp through a wick to a cloth netting that wraps around a ceramic bulb-like object.

The rich *go to* departmental stores, very few in those days: CK Tang, Oriental Emporium, heard of them but never been to any.

The poor *come to* pasar malam: no branding, little differentiation, cheap, price fixes among stalls, low quality, no 'exchange' policy, no 'return' policy, 'what you see is what you get' long before we heard of the WYSIWYG computerese, and buy at your own risk. Customers have to choose for desiring to look different as there was limited supply of one or two pieces of any type, have to check very thoroughly for quality, turn it inside out and outside in if you must. Of course, customers must never open their purses till they have spent fifteen minutes at the very least to drop the vendor's opening price to a quarter of it, and have it taken up in drips until your final price hanged at below half the opening. Even at that level, there was a good probability the vendor fleeced you. Customers must be iron-willed, tough, and strong to handle the haggling, negotiating, and bargaining, shut their ears to all the side talk. They must imagine they were fighting for their lives. Those who survived the pasar malam were generally women folk: they were the toughest people on earth. It is little wonder that women, focused on what they want, get what they want, and get things done. Persistence in pursuit of a goal is in their DNA.

53

Hand-me-downs

I n growing up, we readily accepted hand-me-downs from relatives and neighbours. These came from our uncles the accountant, and the banker. They passed on used pants and shirts to Pa. When I was older and of the right height third uncle's pants fitted me. However, I was too skinny to fit in and Pa had to shorten them and alter the waistline. It looked fine except I felt terribly awkward in them, a young boy trying to fit an adult pants.

Other items we had from our uncles were their children's clothes. Mie made the necessary alterations to salvage them. Sometimes we received seldom-used suitcases, bags, and leather shoes. Used books and toys were always welcome items.

We enjoyed these hand-me-downs, they were generally in good condition, and we appreciated them as 'extras' or bonus.

These hand-me-downs were things we were not able to afford and we made maximum use of them as they were or with alteration and innovation. Pa's maxim was every used thing, every castaway thing had a second life, and he kept that position with unwavering faith.

Within the family, our hand-me-downs were usually school uniforms depending on size. My previous year's uniform went to Cai as a back-up set. Textbooks were also a regular item.

———◆◆◆———

We were grateful for the hand-me-downs. We were thankful to the thoughtful people who gave them to us. It made us appreciate them as showers of blessings. There was no cause to murmur or complain. Receiving them was like a celebration of joy, we would gather to see what goodies were awaiting distribution. As we gathered around, we shared a common happiness, seeing there were the hand-me-downs to share among ourselves, and if something was short, they could be swapped, or modified or altered, such that all benefited.

There was this wonderful sense of deep humility, of exhilarating joy, and of overflowing gratitude. Pa and Mie understood the relief hand-me-downs contributed to our tight purses.

Thrift and frugality are virtues for all times, times of plenty and times of want for the sake of prudence.

Earlier photo: Dressing up for Chinese New Year. Cai and
I wore similar type of clothes bought from the Pasar Malam.

Later photo: Dressing up for Chinese New Year probably
a year later than the preceding photo. The shirt I wore
was an altered 'hand-me-down'. I was also grateful
for my first hand-me-down watch.

54

Dressing Up for CNY

Our clothes were simple: boys had tee shirts and shorts bought from the pasar malam at bargain prices; girls had dresses that Mie sewed from a large piece of pink cloth purchased at a good price as it was plain—no designs, no texture—not usually used to tailor clothes. Still, it was adequately presentable. Mie designed the same pattern with different sizes for all the girls with a simple lace around the front bib-like collar.

For shoes, they came from the pasar malam as well: simple synthetic leather, really more like PVC. Rarely, do we get hand-me-down shoes at that time. When we were older, I wore a hand-me-down pair from youngest uncle, the banker. Still they were too long, and Pa decided to stuff the front with paper he specially packed. That worked just as Pa would have it—everything has a second life!

Once again, common sense and economy were at work. All the girls wore the uniformly designed dresses sewn from the same cloth. Can anyone complain? We boys, Cai and I, had the same tee-shirts,

149

the same shorts, nearly similar shoes. There was little need to be gaudy or glamorous, as long as we look good in them, and they look good on us.

CNY is a special collective celebration of much importance and significance to the Chinese community. It is a celebration of spring, a remembrance of the beginning of the Chinese calendar, a new year after a cold dreary winter. It is a time of joy, life is everywhere, the flowers bloom once again, colours and lightness fill the air. CNY customs and traditions are important. The practices are essential once a year to celebrate as a special occasion. Superstition has it that sweeping on the first day drives away good fortune. Oranges were used in greetings as they brought luck to the recipient; red packets with the right value were issued as in sharing 'fortune'; food such as CNY cookies, roasted pork, pork floss, candies, red dates, and so on added novelty to the festive occasion.

For us, it was a time Pa highlighted our academic achievements to our relatives—we were such diligent students with the best results among our relatives—as we had little else to show.

———❖———

Dressing is necessarily important whether on CNY, any other festivities, or in both formal and informal settings. It serves social and cultural functions and is significant on CNY to respect traditions of our ancestors. It is not to be of sad or mourning colours such as black. Colours should be sprightly preferably bright such as red, vermillion, orange, and yellow. It must be an adornment appropriate to the occasion, reflecting standards of gender, social status, modest, not gaudy. Our dressing for CNY met at least the standards of gender, modesty, and humble/simple enough to mark us out to be presentable of a lower social standing.

Dressing reminds me that when Adam and Eve disobeyed God, they had the knowledge to understand their nakedness and sought to cover themselves with leaves. Our God by His grace and mercy covered them instead with animal skins. Animals were sacrificed to extract the skins. Today we see that God's Son, the perfect Lamb was sacrificed for us and His blood of grace covered us over so that we are reconciled to God for all eternity.

55

Fugitive at the Door

One evening, we were all at home and heard much commotion from one of the eighteen-storey flats. It sounded frightening as though some fighting had gone on, as there was sound of the breaking of glass bottles, overturning of tables and lots of shouting in Malay.

Pa told us to continue with our schoolwork and not be bothered with the goings-on. Soon after ten, all were preparing for bedtime, when Pa looked out the window and immediately told us all to go into the room to sleep. There were several desperate knocks on our main door and Pa kept the security latch on and opened the door to speak to whoever was on the outside. The other spoke in Malay and Pa was able to handle Malay well. Pa then unlatched the door to let the person come in. He was dark skinned and does not look like a Malay, was more Indian. His shirt had large stains of blood. There was a deep gash on his right forearm. Pa shut the door and latched it. He then shut two leaves of our wooden Venetian windows in the living hall. Pa next took him to the back next to the kitchen, sat him down on the floor, and said something to him. Pa then came back with some old cloth and a bottle of solution. Pa cleaned his wounds, applied the solution, and wrapped them with the used cloth. We did not have bandages. That seemed to take care of the bleeding.

He stayed with us for a little while longer until the coast was clear. Pa made sure of that and then opened the door to let him go. The man was grateful and said 'terima kasih' to Pa. That meant 'thank you'.

Pa later explained that a fight had broken out at the coffee shop of the eighteen-storey flats. Beer bottles were broken and groups were involved. It was common for hard-necked workers to gather after work, at coffee shops for dinner and beer. Idle talk allowed these rough people to let off steam about their employers, their supervisors, their work, the government and their policies, women, and anything else that could draw banters from those present. Anything but facts took centrestage. Idle talk and beer-intoxicated minds make poor bedfellows. A harsh word, disagreement, a stare, banging the tables, breaking glass bottles, punch-outs, and in desperation for domination, out came the *parangs* or machetes looking to spill blood.

What good sense can come out of a drunkard with a sodden brain, when his faculties dull, reasoning fail, discernment departed? For the idle talker, his 'drunkenness' springs forth from a mind intolerable of any reasonable converse save his own predispositions, a heart overflowing with passions once brought to heel, now instigated to untamed rage. All beauty shimmers, wavers hesitatingly, and dissipates. Flee from idle conversations as much as possible, for discussion in affairs of the world is a great distraction. We end up trapped and captivated by vanity. From idle talk to disagreement to rage, and to senseless destruction, the sequence was almost predictable.

Pa had been familiar with these roughnecks. His philosophy was to avoid them, never to join them at the coffee shops, to keep away from them. Give no time to them. Yet in this instance, someone needed help badly. Pa would not turn away despite his disgust for such people. More than that, he took in the fugitive, took care of his wounds and hurt, and sent him off safely.

In love is kindness. Kindness is fearless. Fear is often imagined for lack of kindness; judgement fumbles, decisions irresolute, and outcomes ineffective.

Endnotes

This reminds me of the parable of The Good Samaritan, paraphrased below.

Jesus replied, "A man was going down from Jerusalem to Jericho, and he fell among robbers, who stripped him and beat him and departed, leaving him half dead.

Now by chance a priest was going down that road, and when he saw him, he passed by on the other side. So likewise, a Levite, when he came to the place and saw him, passed by on the other side. But a Samaritan as he journeyed, came to where he was, and when he saw him, he had compassion. He went to him and bound up his wounds, pouring on oil and wine. Then he set him on his own animal, and brought him to an inn and took care of him. And the next day he took out two denarius and gave them to the innkeeper, saying, "Take care of him, and whatever more you spend, I will repay you when I come back."

Which of these three, do you think, proved to be a neighbour, to the man who fell among the robbers?

It is the sufferer, wherever, whoever, whatsoever he be. Wherever you hear the cry of distress, wherever you see anyone sent to cross your path by the Providence of God, whom it is in your power to help—whether stranger or enemy—*he* is your neighbour.

56

Trip to Johor Prison

Johor the southernmost state of Malaya across from the northern part of Singapore has a long history of close affinity with us. A narrow three-quarter mile strip of water called the Straits of Singapore separates us and we cross over by means of a causeway.

Monthly on Saturday morning, Pa would arrange for a large Mercedes car driven by a Malay chauffeur to take us to the Johor prison. It was a long drive to the prison. The car was large enough to accommodate Pa, Mie, and five children. We would wind down the windows with the chauffeur's permission to let the wind flow over and caress our faces. The feeling was of calm and coolness in the mid morning sun, and offered a joyful sensation of unbounded freedom.

We arrived at the gates of the Johor State Prison and the chauffeur stopped the car just outside. Pa spoke to the chauffeur in Malay and we all waited while Pa took over from Mie a tall light brown paper bag containing Brylcreem hair cream, Colgate toothpaste, toothbrush, Pigeon soap, and other toiletries. We stayed outside the prison gate and Pa went in alone.

It was something like over fifteen minutes before Pa appeared at the gate. The chauffeur had a chat with Pa and he drove us to a very large pineapple plantation to visit the owner of the Mercedes car. He also owned several plantations in Johor. We had pineapple drinks, met the family, and went to watch fishes in a pool. The place had large areas of lush rolling greens but the house fronted by a row of tall consistent casuarinas, was ordinary and jaded in comparison. The estate was that of the Chuan Seng family. Courtesies adequately extended Pa took leave, and we returned home to Singapore.

———◆———

Pa visited two Thai nationals arrested by the Malayan police in Johor. Pa came to learn of them from the Thai Buddhist temple at Silat Road. Their families had sought the temple for help and the temple turned to Pa. The pineapple plantation owner had been an irregular temple devotee and Pa knew them. The owner was very generous in providing the transportation and allowing us to visit.

Pa never revealed what the prisoners were in custody for. As with Pa, he waved off our prying questions and we understood it to mean the end of further questions on the matter. The toiletries Pa brought to them were a kindness extended on our family's budget that Pa gladly acceded. The future Johor trips also benefited us when we visited the zoo and other places there.

———◆———

A prison in our minds was a bad place where evil and wicked people remained as punishment for their misdeeds. It was difficult to understand at that time why Pa should be involved with them. It was as we found out, about kindness, and about kinship of fellow Thai compatriots.

As with the 'fugitive at the door', Pa extended aid to anyone in need. It was always about the person in need regardless of our circumstances and substance. It was never about the transgression the person had committed, or that he had brought it upon himself and therefore deserving of punishment.

We are here to serve, not served.

We must always consider the issue at hand and not the person. *The heart is deceitful above all things, and desperately sick; who can understand it?*

The LORD searches the heart and test the mind, to give every man according to his ways, according to the fruit of his deeds.

Botanic Gardens Outing a day after Chinese New Year,
I was on far right, next in the front row was my cousin, Fong,
daughter of uncle in the Tiong Bahru kampong. Pa was not
in the picture as he had a prior appointment. Photo shot by
Mie's younger brother who was a photography enthusiast

Another Botanic Gardens Outing shot,
notice the girls' dressing, all cut from the same
light pink cloth. Mie tailored them.

57

Botanic Gardens Outing

W e had an outing to the Singapore Botanic Gardens a day after Chinese New Year. It was a lovely day, neither too sunny nor humid. Mie's younger brother, whose wife was the roving hairdresser, took us there in a borrowed small pick-up truck. As in the photo in the preceding page, we numbered ten including uncle (not in photo) and Fong my cousin whose father lived at Tiong Bahru kampong. Pa did not join us that morning as he had a prior appointment to attend.

The Gardens was a public place and we did not have to pay an entrance charge. Mie took along water and sandwiches enough for all. It was the sort of outing intended to while away the time on the festive Chinese New Year occasion when there was not much to do than visitations; take photos, stroll or run about freely in the expanse of the Gardens. We were watchful to maintain our dressing and presentation, and hence refrained from running.

Such formal outings were rare other than those to the Johor State Prison. This was a formal leisurely outing during a festivity, looking neat and being well dressed was necessary. It was a bit of a 'stiff-collared' activity except we did not have collars on our tee shirts, an outing not immensely enjoyable but culturally necessary.

Today there are a lot more options on a festivity outing and they are certainly relaxing and casual ones. Outings gave us something to talk about when asked 'what did you do during Chinese New Year?' It was a good thing to have made at least one outing wherever it was. It offered normality in life, a customary thing to do . . . an expectation. Alas! Life was an expectation, someone else's expectation, cultural norm, societal order. Today, society fights the norms and conducts itself with much liberty free from the constraints of the 'stiff-collared' past. Yet we sometimes are nostalgic for what the past mean—an anchor to history, a tether to respect, and to deference—while today life is as driftwood floated in the streaming currents of existentialist materialism, no reference to pride and value of times past. Life had a reference point to which we moved back and forth in adjustment with consideration of family, of relationships, of love, and attention. Much of it now rests in the self, in the acquisition of personal well-being that qualifies one to go on the chessboard of life.

In those early days, there was an expected sense of posing well whenever we took a photo. There was a sense of order, of hierarchy, of how it ought to be. Everyone would look into the camera, not too serious, not too out-of-control, looking one's best. Photo taking was a formal activity. Over the years that had changed, these days the subjects smile almost as a requirement when the photographer tells them to 'say cheese'. Sometimes, subjects make funny signs and portray their lighter sides, the 'candid' perspective, and the preferred natural look.

Changing times reflect the moderated attitudes even to a simple thing as photo taking. Cameras were rare then and considered expensive to own. These days they are ubiquitous. They feature in our mobile phones, i-tablets, and on our notebook computers. Their quality and capabilities have improved by leaps, and bounds from the large bulky old cameras. Their portability, instant production, their ease of copying and sharing had run deep furrows through our natural lives, and change our appreciation of what a capture of the 'moment of truth' is like.

58

Aquarium: Hobby to Chore

A neighbour friend gave us a fish bowl with guppies in it, some white sand and a few strands of seaweeds. We were all excited and when Pa got home from work, he added to the little pandemonium that went on. He said he would get a gold fish the next day.

We progressed from goldfish in a bowl to a small rectangular fish tank with a frontal glass window and a larger tank and to two large tanks. Pa bred Black Mollies that he sold, some he traded for rare guppies and so on. More types of fishes came on the scene: zebras, sucker mouths, angels, swordtails, tetras, gouramis, and so on. Pa wanted to breed them, bring about reproduction, and soon whenever a pregnant fish was due, we would prepare the nets ready to separate the babies from the larger fish. There were times the larger fishes ate the babies. The birth was quite a sight as each baby came out of the mother's womb. Each birth provided an easy dozen babies. Those were exciting moments as our task was to fish out the babies into a bottle or smaller tank if available. There were times when Pa was at work and the big responsibility fell on us to keep things under control.

The initial cleaning was easy with the goldfish bowl. The small rectangular tank was manageable. When the large tank made its appearance, we drew the dirty water using tubes that required us to suck it and quickly allow the water to run on its own flow. Often, we ended up having dirty water in our mouths, and the feeling was nasty. Occasionally the smaller less valuable fishes came out and ran off into the sinkhole. There was much explanation required and Pa would show his irritation at our lack of concentration. With the big tank, we had to move the fishes out to smaller containers while we scrubbed the tank. Some of those frightful or energetic fishes jumped out of the nets and were jumping on dry floor. We thought they might die or ended up maimed or something. We learned there was little to fear about their condition as long as we quickly moved them back to water.

It was hours long of standing and working through them, Pa, Cai, and I were involved. Eventually we withdrew from fish rearing and Pa continued with it for a long time, alone. Pa did not fuss about it as we had other tasks that took priority mostly centred about schoolwork. Occasionally, Pa would get us to help not because he needed the help. I suspect it was mostly to get us back into it: rearing aquarium fish can be rather lonely for Pa.

What started as an enjoyable hobby ended a burdensome chore. Delight converted to drudgery. What once started as a small simple hobby had become too large for our interest, the tasks of maintaining it too unpleasant, and the effort too time consuming. The hobby had become a 'monster' and grown beyond our initial fancy. Our young lively minds had little patience just watching incommunicable fishes swim about in their own world. For Pa it was different. He worked through it with zealous commitment that was past our understanding.

Where there is no vision, the people perish. We did not have a vision about fish rearing, our whim for it died. Pa had a vision and persisted at rearing fish on his own. After a long time that vision also died, it was neither compelling nor enduring.

59

Politics: Merger, Confrontation, Separation

S oldiers were running along the blocks of flats with rifles and butting anyone who put out their heads. Before this, sirens went off, there were some vehicles with loud hailers announcing that the curfew was effective immediately and no one should be on the streets. I had no understanding of why we should have a curfew that kept us indoors.

I remembered another occasion at the Thai temple in Silat, where from the grilled window I caught a momentary glimpse of Mr. Lee Kuan Yew, our Prime Minister. The crowd was thick, with much jostling, and he was visiting the worship hall as part of his political tour. There was much political activity as this during this time.

In early 1965, we watched on TV news that a building, MacDonald House in Orchard Road had been bombed. It was the work of Indonesian terrorists.

Later that same year on TV, I saw Mr. Lee interviewed about separation from Malaysia. This time he was sombre and emotional. It was as though all the clamour, excitement, and bustle took a downturn. He talked about the separation and publicly shed tears in front of the whole nation.

Indonesia, then under Sukarno's presidency had opposed the union of Malaysia, Sabah, Sarawak, and Singapore. It adopted a policy of confrontation against Malaysia, meaning the union of the four countries. The policy known as 'Konfrontasi' lasted from 1963 to 1966 aimed at disrupting the merger, and terrorist activities occurred in the four countries. In Singapore, the MacDonald House bombing was notable. Konfrontasi ended when Sukarno lost power at the end of 1965.

The merger of the four states to form Malaysia in 1963 did not last and Mr. Lee's vision that Singapore was/must be part of Malaysia ended in 1965. That was also Singapore's emergence as an independent nation to fend for herself.

A Confrontation driven by the imagined political ideology of Sukarno against a Merger of four generally diverse states with deep historical/cultural differences and political agendas less than coherent or integrated must necessarily end in Separation.

Those were heady days, politics just as wild, socio-economic conditions less than favourable, and the players far idealistic and untested in young nationhood.

Separation, as I think back, had been good for us. It forced us out of our imagined fear of what could be. We had no choice but to work to ensure we do not let our fear be. This has been much like the rollercoaster in our lives with its attendant lows and highs. *To everything, there is a season and a time to every purpose under the heaven.*

Merger was a time to embrace, and
Separation a time to refrain from embracing.

Separation was a time to break down, and
Independence a time to build up.

Mr. Lee on national TV was a time to weep.
Today is a time to gratefully, and humbly smile (laugh).

Who oversaw them all? Our Lord, God Almighty saw them all, what politicians, and rulers may think and ponder, our God has the last say. They wanted merger, went through it, and failed. Sukarno's Konfrontasi met its end when other events transpired. We did not ask for Independence but God saw it would be good, we got it and it stayed.

Hear what Nebuchadnezzar, the greatest and most powerful of Babylonian kings had to say of our God: "*Now I Nebuchadnezzar praise and extol and honour the King of heaven, all whose works are truth, and his ways judgment: and those that walk in pride he is able to abase.*"

Endnotes

Let every soul be subject unto the higher powers. For there is no power but of God: the powers that be are ordained of God. Whosoever therefore resisteth the power, resisteth the ordinance of God: and they that resist shall receive to themselves damnation. For rulers are not a terror to good works, but to the evil. Wilt thou then not be afraid of the power?

60

My Secret Sweetheart

In my fourth year, a new girl joined my class. Most other students were from the third year and gained promotion to the fourth. This new girl was not new. She had always been with the school but was in a different session. For the fourth year, her parents had requested for a change in session. The school had a morning and afternoon session.

Her name was Lin and she was pretty and pleasant. I liked her. She had poise, was lively, spoke clearly, graceful, without temper, and very much at ease with herself. We interacted much as we sat next to each other, and after many months, I thought I would like her for a wife. We really got along very well.

———————❧———————

Lin's parents operated a vegetable stall at the market. I checked it out on a Saturday morning when we did not have school. I was also on an errand for Mie. I saw Lin helped her mother, who was much older than Mie and a rather large woman. Lin was Cantonese. She was the youngest in her family.

At school, Lin was a diligent student. She ranked within the top 10 when we were in the fourth grade at Jervois East. Her writing was bold and neat, very organised and sure. There were days when we fought over some childish things like pencils and erasers—all part of children's whims and fancies—and she would ignore me. As soon as I apologised we were back on terms. We had a great time all the way until the sixth grade.

———◆———

I had no idea as to what a wife meant, other than someone you lived with, and who gave you children the way Mie was to Pa—a child's simple notion. For me it was someone I enjoyed passing my days with, and even after a disagreement, we comfortably patched back the next day just as Lin and I had on several occasions. Of course, we were just classmates and friends. Lin was my first and only sweetheart through my life until I met my wife in my 'brooding' years.

The husband-wife relationship that Mie and Pa had was a significant and enduring example of what marriages ought to be. Mie stuck with Pa through 'thick and thin', to have and to hold, in good times and in bad, in sickness and in health, for better or for worse, for richer or for poorer, to love and to cherish, till parted by death. They lived through the difficult and testing times, physically as well as emotionally. Nearly five decades later, when Pa passed away at eighty-one, Mie followed suit a month later.

Endnotes

Childhood sweethearts are just that, however, they give us a preview of the *innocence* seen also in another child of the opposite sex. That preview is a mirror of our self. It tells me of what I saw as a fit in the other's nature and character. As I thought about it, more and more the preview tells me clearly of the type of person I wished to have as a close companion for life.

Lin passed out of my view after the age of innocence. However, the imprint of her nature and character stayed on in my mind.

Will time change that innocent image at that age of innocence?

Only a heart after God's own is what we must look out for, in ourselves, in those we befriend, and in our life partner.

61

Haemoglobin for Coca-Cola

M r. Pereira, our Science teacher was a young man in his late twenties, walked into class and told us that the lesson for day was to be on the blood circulation system. After the lesson, he gave us something *extra* that was not in the textbook. Apart from the basic things that we knew like blood vessels (arteries, veins, capillaries), blood and its composition of red and white corpuscles, platelets and the like, he said that the blood carried oxygen for distribution to the rest of the body. He explained that the blood had haemoglobin made up of an iron atom to which was attached four nitrogen atoms that allowed the oxygen atom to attach. As a quiz with a reward of a bottle of Coca-Cola, he wanted us to spell haemoglobin. We had never seen or heard of this word until his mention that day. It was fun, a long word. Nearly half the class tried and all got it wrong. I raised my hand and asked Mr. Pereira to pronounce it again slowly. I then tried it: H-A-E-M-O-G-L-O-B-I-N. He smiled and let the class know that the spelling was perfect. He took out fifteen cents from his pocket and asked me to go to the canteen to buy and bring up the Coca-Cola. When I returned, he took it from me and officially presented it to me. The class applauded and Mr. Pereira allowed me to drink from the bottle with a straw.

Spelling was usually easy and depended on sounds and familiarity. Of course, today we have 'spelling bee' contests and the like. In Jervois East, we never had any such contests. However, we had a weekly written spelling 'practice' where we memorised ten words and as the form teacher read out the words, we wrote it in the Spelling exercise book for marking. In the higher grades, we had Dictation of sentences and not merely individual words.

There was an element of memory and I often thought that was not the key to being a 'spelling bee'. Today we have phonics, the method of teaching reading and spelling based on phonetic interpretation of ordinary spelling. I listened to the pronunciation (sound of the word) and then spelled from it. It was phonics in practice. We learned phonics subconsciously through regular exposure to reading aloud, spelling and recitation.

I was sure at the end of that lesson I did not replace my blood and its haemoglobin for Coca Cola. Coca Cola got as far as my gut and out with the 'drafts'. I wished Mr. Pereira had given us more such quizzes, with or without the Coca Cola. Still, Coca Cola provided the 'fizz'.

Endnotes

Mr. Pereira was an innovative teacher with a love for teaching. He never made himself too familiar with the students and kept a certain distance, but occasionally I caught a half smile coming on his face as he turned away from the class to write something on the green chalkboard. He never looked at the class to flash a smile. I sensed he enjoyed the students in his class. He often quizzed us about things outside of the school textbook curriculum. For us, the perpetually inquisitive lot, we enjoyed his teaching.

62

My Voice . . . my voice

I t was in primary five and I was a member in the choir. At the last quarter of the year, I realized my sweet voice was going low and I sounded weird. At home, Mie and my siblings joked that I sounded like a duck. It seemed to get worse. I avoided speaking. One day there was to be intensive choir training and practices to prepare for a public performance in a month. That meant we would each have to sing individually for the choirmaster to correct us. With a voice like mine, I was unable to face this humiliation. Just before the practice, I decided I would not attend on the pretext of being unwell.

That was the age of puberty. It was frightening suddenly to be unable to retain one's voice. I skipped the choir practice with the excuse of being unwell, and quietly left the choir for good. I became a little withdrawn from speaking, even when at home. The year-end school holidays had arrived and I was hopeful of an improvement in my voice. It never quite happened even though I privately attempted to work on restoring it. Well, as in most things, I got used to it, and others became familiar with it and life went on as though I never had an earlier different voice.

Sudden change can often be completely disarming. It takes us by surprise and alienates us from understanding and accepting it. Withdrawal from our environment follows, sometimes for good and at other times, may lead to isolation. I was blessed to have the school holidays to heal from the sudden change, to understand that I was unable to do anything about it, and know that many others go through such a condition, some more drastic and others less so.

I did not lose my voice rather I found a new voice that stood me well to good effect. I went on to read the Malay *pantun* (poetry) before the whole school. I was in a class debating team at fourteen, you may think of it as a one-time debater. As an adult in business, I have stood before and spoken to large groups of employees, conducted training, led seminars for chief executives, promoted national business programs and the like. They were in a way efforts at purging the fear of the voice change.

Losses are often disguised gains.

The first shall be last, and the last shall be first.

63

P-r-e-f-e-c-t . . . near perfect

I had been class monitor for several years at different grades. From the fourth grade, I often wondered what qualified one to be a school prefect. A school prefect had to wear a neat tie that was hooked on the shirt collar and made him or her look smart. Teachers had to select the prefect and have the headmaster's agreement. A prefect's qualifications remained unknown to me. From my observation, they were normally the taller and bigger boys. Academically, they never ranked at the top few in their class but were generally within the top half. They were not trouble—makers and were obedient.

In my mind, I had always disqualified myself as I was rather 'small' in stature and was a malnourished boy. It came as a complete surprise when at the end of my fifth year at Jervois East the headmaster informed me that teachers had selected me to be a school prefect when school started the following year. Presented to me, was a deep blue tie with the school insignia embroidered on the front. I felt much pride and honour. Pa and Mie would be overwhelmed.

I found out from my teacher that among other things, my academic performance, bearing, and good conduct, which probably meant helpfulness, obedience, willingness to participate during lessons, responsive and the like, enabled me to qualify to be a prefect.

A school prefect had duties such as:

- waiting at the school gate to take down names of students who were late for school,
- taking turns to raise and lower the school's and national flags,
- warning students caught littering and
- enforce overall cleanliness in the school compound.

I particularly loved the latter activities of running about purposefully to get students to pick up litter they failed to notice or pretended they missed. They gave the Speedy Gonzales in me an opportunity to get 'to the rescue'.

One does not have to be perfect to be a school prefect. There was this sense of merit, fulfilment, of dignity, of honour and importance. Appointment to school prefect was a reward for academic performance and personal bearing/conduct that sets a shining example for the rest of the school to follow/emulate. There was a required devotion to the senior role of leading the younger students to uphold the school's motto of Joint Effort for Success, derived from the JES short form of Jervois East School. I truly valued and cherished the experience.

Endnotes

A prefect's role is that of servant leadership, the kind we see in our Lord Jesus. He came to serve. Our role of leadership should model after our Lord and Master.

64

Teacher's Pet

It was the high level of activity and involvement, as class monitor, school prefect, that made me stand out. The heightened competition and my responsiveness during lessons afforded me a high profile in class. Visibly my form master Mr. Heng was excited and very soon made me an unannounced favourite of his. He would always put me in charge of activities or got me to do things for him at the office as he found me to be highly reliable and capable.

Noticeably, he held high expectations on me to continue to perform and take on additional responsibilities. It became clear I was Mr. Heng's blue-eyed boy. He looked lightly on much of my schoolwork, encouraged me on every turn, and showed me off to other teachers. I did not enjoy the tag of favourite of Mr Heng.

Two years before I was also a favourite of the woman form teacher, Miss Chia. She handled me quite differently from Mr. Heng. She did not fall all over me but was very clear and direct in her instructions. Occasionally I might receive a harsh word for a deviation.

I enjoyed the approach better than Mr. Heng's. She did not make her favouritism emphatically obvious and yet I was able to understand, enjoy, and appreciate her estimate of me. I valued her preference better.

Mr. Heng's esteem of me seemed directed to himself; he favoured me, as he felt proud of me for his student. That was my sense of it.

There is a thin line in the manner favouritism is handled so that it did not have to come across as such. It is in giving that we receive, that was like Miss Chia. You will read in chapter 69 that my position in Miss Chia's watch was 7 out of 70. With Mr Heng, my sense was he received and liked what he received, and therefore he gave on that basis. My position under his watch was 1 out of 168. Still, I am most grateful for both their estimates of me as a young lad. Both thought I was hardworking and helpful.

The wonderful sense of the loving esteem from my teachers for the reasons mentioned was highly motivating, like a silent, persistent, gentle nudge working all the time to get you on top of everything you lay your hands on. It is still a grade lower than the love of Pa and Mie.

65

Reciting the pantun (poetry)

My form teacher summoned me to his office about one month before the school's 'prize giving' day. I was to read a Malay poem or *pantun*. He said I would have to stand before the whole school to recite it, better still if I would memorize it. He handed me a piece of paper with the *pantun* on it. I was afraid the whole school might not hear a tiny voice like mine. To allay my fear, he said I would stand on a chair that placed on a large writing desk and that he would have someone hold up a loud hailer for me to speak.

When the day arrived, it all happened as planned. I delivered the *pantun* well and received a pat from the principal.

———◆———

I was top student for Malay. We used to call it *Bahasa Kebangsaan*, the Malay word for National Language. English was the first language and Chinese was my second language. Reciting the *pantun* was not a problem at all. Since Malay was Romanised using the English letters and sounds, it was easy to pronounce and learn.

There was a particular line in the poem that I seemed to remember to this day. It went something like that: *Kalau malu, mungkin lapar.* What it meant was that 'if shy, hunger necessarily follows'.

That was my first public speaking assignment albeit a prepared 'speech'. There was hardly any stage fright and it was attributable to the age of innocence as well as familiarity with the language.

Kalau malu, mungkin lapar left quite an impression on me and may have had a subconscious imprint just as a lot of other experiences had on how I conducted myself in life. I will ask when in need or doubt. I will search for answers to problems when they come forth, I will tread gently in uncertainties.

Endnotes

Ask, and it shall be given you; *seek,* and ye shall find; *knock,* and it shall be opened unto you.

Hear; for I will speak of excellent things.

66

My Eyes

At the year's end after the examinations, there was a day of health screening for the eye, teeth, and the measuring of weight and height. When it came to my turn to check the eye, a card covered one eye and then the other while the nurse pointed out the alphabets and numbers on a wall chart for me to read. I was unable to read all of them. A prescription instructed me to visit any outside optician to get a pair of glasses. I kept the prescription and did not let Pa know about it.

I was afraid a pair of glasses would burden Pa financially. I would be in secondary school the following year and the expenses were likely to go up much in school fees, in transport, and meals.

Although I was thoughtful of our family's financial condition, the deferment in correcting my short sightedness early on created problems for me in secondary school when the condition worsened and affected my grades. *My dilemma was concerning the duty to deny myself of or indulge in the pair glasses.* I chose the former for reasons mentioned thinking I could manage a little while without glasses as long I was seeing well enough to get about my reading and daily functioning.

As for the light of mine eyes, it also is gone from me.—Psalms 38:10

I certainly lacked the wisdom to deal with the problem. You could say I was short sighted in my short sightedness with the consequence of a worsening short sightedness.

"Wisdom . . . the art of reaching one's end by the use of the right means." (Smend)

67

Top Boy

My sixth year at Jervois East capped my primary education at a regular neighbourhood school. It was a year of excitement with preparation for the Primary School Leaving Examinations, school prefect duties, class monitor duties, and a silent attention from my form teacher on a select few to outperform. There was no extra/special coaching but simply an overt expectation from teachers for the few to lift school honours. Competition was intense between me and another boy, and in the final school examinations, I got the better of him for the crown of top student. I had First prizes in English, Mathematics, History, Geography, and Malay. There was also a prize for topping the whole school.

Prizes were mostly books and games. Prizewinners chose their prizes from a pool of books and games about two weeks before the Prize-giving Day. I have received prizes in as many years at Jervois East but never before so many prizes at one time. They were as gifts for which I did not have to pay.

Prizes felt like one earned them; in this case, through excellent performance. It was as though I ran a race and in winning it, I received a crown. Prizes were *rewards* for the performer's efforts.

I considered them *gifts* as well simply because I received them free of any charge, and in freely a manner. Gifts were *recognition* of the giver's joy in the performer's efforts.

Endnotes

Our Maker *gifted* us our salvation. We have to work out our salvation, to ". . . press toward the mark for the *prize* of the high calling . . ."

Know ye not that they which run in a race run all, but one receiveth the prize? So run, that ye may obtain.

68

To the Top Secondary School

This was the second half of December of the year (1967) I was in primary six. We had selected the first and second choices of schools we desired postings to, all based on the PSLE (Primary School Leaving Examinations) results. We had completed the PSLE earlier on in November.

That day came for the announcement of the results and the school to which we each go. The primary six students gathered at the school tuck shop. The place was simply abuzz with students all excited guessing where they would go, others laughing away, some forlorn, believing they had not done well, yet still others went around to collect signatures/parting words for their autograph books.

The headmaster stood up a large office desk with a loud hailer in his right hand and an opened file with his left hand. He spoke and almost instantaneously, the buzzing came to an unsolicited halt. A complete silence filled the air. All eyes were on the headmaster. He called out the students' names in class order. They queued in the front to collect their report books containing the results of the examinations and the school posting.

My class was next, several names called, and then mine was next. I went forward with great expectation, collected my report book, and moved hurriedly to a corner, flipping quickly to the last few pages to look for the result and school posting entries. I found them. I did well . . . very well. My school posting was to RAFFLES INSTITUTION! Yes! It was the school of choice and I was going there! Pa and Mie were so proud of this achievement.

My friends huddled around, exchanged report books to view the results, congratulated each other, commiserated with one another, and this went on until all report books were issued. Some of us went about to thank the teachers for their love, guidance and patience, before we headed for home.

One other boy from my class went to RI short for Raffles Institution with me. RI was the oldest school in Singapore and was at that time the top secondary as well, a school that had produced the President, Prime Minister, various Ministers, and famous people from all strata of life. It was a government school and therefore a public school, taking in students based on the merit of their academic performances. It was a school for the rich and poor to study and compete, based on effort and ability. It was a proud place to be educated in. The name itself spoke of brilliance, character, excellence, energy, public service in every age. RI well known for its sports achievements in athletics, gymnastics, football, rugby, softball, hockey, volleyball, etc., was an all-rounded school of excellence.

Pa and Mie were so proud that I could sense they were anxious to see me make good right through my first year at RI. That was enough to have them rethink plans and priorities. Pa worked hard at his job as fitter and an evening job as bartender to a British military club, and Mie as an amah to English-speaking foreigners.

At that time, there was a sense of nostalgia when we left Jervois East School knowing we would go into another phase of education, likely to be different from where we were leaving. Still, it was a challenge to experience and welcome. I felt like I was to miss the teachers and friends I have made in the past six years. I would miss the place that symbolised fun.

Jervois East was fun:
Where I ran freely in wide and open spaces,
Where I caught spiders,
Where I reared frogs through their life cycle as a science project,
Where I waded through a flood,
Where I saw a bomb,
Where I met a sweetheart,
Where I was class monitor for several years,
Where I became prefect though not near perfect,
Where I collected many prizes for doing well,
Where I was a spelling bee,
Where I was the teachers' favourite,
Where, before the whole school I recited a pantun.
Now, the race is run, my prize finally won,
A Future promised, a bigger Beyond.
Jervois East . . . I must now leave.
Raffles Institution, . . . to you I now come.

Jervois East was a place where I grew up in and thrived, a place that tested me against the standards of the education system and in turn the cultural-socio-economic system. The testing was a preparation for another phase of education until we spin off from the system. Education is only one area—a major one—among others that impinges on our lives and what ultimately we become.

The husbandman that labours must be first partaker of the fruits.

Ye shall know them by their fruits.

69

Report Book Comments

W hen in primary school, that is, from age 6+ to 12, I have always enjoyed the Form Master's Report in the report book. Below is an extract from primary one all the way to primary 6 of such 'remarks'. They gave me sense of how I was performing and how I ought to conduct myself. There was encouragement in them, warnings notwithstanding when the grades fell. The Form Master's Report was hand written by the form teacher in his own hand and was typically with a fountain pen.

Pr. 1A Year 1962
1st Term: Tends to be too over-confident in his work. [*The subject grades were simply 'good', 'fair', or 'fairly good'*]
2nd Term: Could have done better. [*Position was 24 out of 42*]
3rd Term: Well done! Keep it up! [*Position was 6 out of 84*]

Pr. 2A Year 1963
1st Term: A hardworking and helpful pupil. [*Position was 9 out of 41*]
2nd Term: Satisfactory work. [*Position was 9 out of 81*]
3rd Term: Well done! Keep up the good work! [*Position was 3 out of 79*]

Pr. 3B Year 1964

1st Term: Has done his best, well behaved. [*Position was 2 out of 39*]

2nd Term: Keep it up. [*Position was 1 out of 39*]

3rd Term: Slackened. Work harder. [*Position was 7 out of 74*]

Pr. 4B Year 1965

1st Term: An industrious pupil, helpful in class. [*Position was 6 out of 37*]

2nd Term: A conscientious worker, a reliable boy. [*Position was 7 out of 71*]

3rd Term: Hardworking and diligent. Keep up the spirit of working! [*Position was 7 out of 70*]

Pr. 5B Year 1966

1st Term: A steady worker having a spirit of willingness. [*Position was 2 out of 36*]

2nd Term: Well done! [*Position was 1 out of 67*]

3rd Term: Keep it up! [*Position was 2 out of 68*]

Pr. 6A Year 1967

1st Term: [there were no formal tests]

2nd Term: Well done! Keep it up! . . . A modest, and hardworking pupil. [*Position was 1 out of 83*]

3rd Term: Has shown very good work throughout the year, a helpful lad. [*Position was 1 out of 168*]

In some school terms, the position was the ranking in the class while in some cases they were the ranking of two classes at that level in one session. There were two sessions—morning and afternoon—per level. Generally, there were two classes in each session. The exception was in primary six when the classes in both sessions counted to identify the position ranking at the school level.

Form masters had quite a fair bit of work to do with the Report Books. Fountain pens were the writing instrument for official documents. I really liked pens; the imprints were permanent unlike pencils. There was also a style about it. Children used only pencils until they were ten years old, the fourth grade, when they began to use fountain pens for cursive handwriting. Before that time, our writing was in straight form.

When Pa and I first saw the word 'over-confident' in the primary one first term report, we simply did not understand. We went to Pa's dictionary, looked up 'over-confident', but could not find it. After some discussion, we agreed to try 'confident' and found it. Pa read off the Thai meaning and tried explaining to me in Fujian. I caught an idea of it and tried working on being more *careful* with my schoolwork from that point on.

We never had any access to the Report Book except those terms when we had tests and the Form Master's Report when they required our parent/guardian to sign off as evidence that they had viewed the child's performance at school. For Pa and me the Report Book was something we looked forward to every term. It gave Pa an idea of my performance relative to other children, what subjects I was not good in, and so on. Simply it was a measure of how my school life was going. I really thought it was a great tool much like 'lead' and 'lag' scorecards used in business and government to assess what *had* happened and to highlight what *could be* happening. They are much like the dials/meters we have in the car or the very many gauges we see in an aircraft cockpit. They are necessary to the driver and the pilot for safe navigation on the journey.

Our fervour and progress in all that we put our hands to must increase day by day. We cannot claim of any lack.

Whatsoever your hand finds to do, do *it* with your might; for *there is* no work, nor device, nor knowledge, nor wisdom, in the grave, where you go.

The light of the eyes rejoiceth the heart: *and* a good report maketh the bones fat.

EPILOGUE

—◆—

We *begun* with my first memory: little baby brother permanently *adopted out* with little to remember of him. We *ended* with memory of six great years from Jervois East as I *departed* to new challenges.

What begun shall end: perfected, completed, and concluded. Yet, as the *Age of Innocence* shuts its door behind me, the door to the *Age of Discovery* opens and beckons. I must enter.

The events are like puzzle pieces that I have attempted to put together in an organised manner in clock time. Its aim is to let them build for themselves the story of my life between ages three and twelve, in the *age of innocence*.

Much of the book centred on Pa and Mie who worked to earn an income, managed expenses, and directed the conduct of our household. The book also focused on schoolwork as a form of Pa's and Mie's hopes and dreams for the family. The reported events provided access to the web of relationships of family, friends, educators, and the society-at-large.

In the Age of Innocence, I realised all the events have provided my young life a sense of what people do with their lives—their comings and goings, their conducts and behaviours, their beliefs, preferences, predispositions, their dreams and hopes—and finally their *doings* that define their commitments. What one sows, one reaps. The cause-and-effect idea is pervasive. In reflecting, I realised at that age I made no conclusion about those events and the experiences they brought to bear upon my life. My mind had not taken up a model of life it was still learning and needed to discover more. The experiences were taken in and passed through a sieve to the next Age of Discovery.

In your reading of this book up until now, you have participated in its story line and I hope you have seen a *concept* of life, your life. Perhaps you might wish to write your own life.

Milton said it best when on his twenty-third birthday he wrote:

Yet be it less or more, or soon or slow,
It shall be still in strictest measure even
To that same lot, however mean or high,
Toward which Time leads me, and the will of Heaven.
All is, if I have grace to use it so,
As ever, in my great Taskmaster's eye.

Innocence is a state of simplicity, sincerity, an absence of guile or cunning, naiveté. It appears to be so, as I end here and had started to frame the follow-on books. At least for now, it appears innocence lie on the verge of a concentric continuum of our lives that leads to . . . *discovery* . . . *restlessness* . . . and to *brooding*. Will all this lead to a better Robin Blessed? Will the continuum take an upward growth path or will it turn down for the worse? Is it all just a rollercoaster? Find that out in my next book, ***Age of Discovery***. It still does not end there.

A word of comfort from our Lord and Master that bids us consider Him.

"All that the Father giveth me shall come to me; and him that cometh to me I will in no wise cast out."

A NOTE TO READERS

F or readers who have enjoyed this first book of mine, Age of INNOCENCE, you may wish to look out for the next book, Age of DISCOVERY in your local bookstores or on www. amazon.com due out in a few months.

Any comments, suggestions, and communication you wish to have with the author may be directed to: blessedprobin@gmail.com

ACKNOWLEDGEMENTS

I owe all to my Creator, who made all things; *and without him was not anything made that was made.*

My Creator had given me Pa and Mie who have been excellent parents despite their limitations, which they overcame through simple, wise, practical means, centred in love. They were also my 'teachers' in life. The subject they specialised in was 'LOVE'. Most distinctive was their love through their 'walk'. As accomplished saints, they have passed on into glory.

Special Thanks must go to my youngest sister, Tina for contributing the photos used in this book without prior knowledge of this writing project. She is the family's faithful repository of photos. She worked on them in spite of her allergy to dust.

Special Thanks I accord also to Daniel my son, who worked on the old photos in my possession that Tina did not have. In spite of an extremely busy schedule and a 'huge' workload, he made time for dad.

Thanks also belong to the team at Trafford Publishing for patience and persistence to get the book published with quality and on time. Trafford has a simple and proven system to help first-time authors such as me to start right making their work and mine more efficient and productive.

Thanks can only silently pass to all those who have been a part of my life, a list of which is much too long to produce here. Many have gone to their own places, and many others still alive may never know about the existence of this book.

ABOUT THE AUTHOR

The author is semi-retired and is an executive coach. Trained as an accountant in industry, he has been a senior manager, management consultant, trainer, seminar leader, financial advisor, and blog publisher. The author is married, with two adult children and a granddaughter, and lives in Singapore. He worships at a Bible-believing church. The author writes under a pen name.

The author believes that life is not accidental but has a purposeful design privy only to the Creator. He catches glimpses of it as he reflects on his own life. Time reveals a coherence of all of life's *past* events as he sees them dovetailed or integrated into the ultimate divine purpose.

This book is the first of a planned sequel that seeks to understand a *concept* of life by reflecting on logical stages of development, and revealing the completed part of the divine blueprint as he sees it.